1000 Only Fools and Horses Facts

Ben Wharton

© Copyright 2024 Ben Wharton
All Rights Reserved

CONTENTS

4 - Introduction
5 - 1000 Only Fools and Horses Facts

INTRODUCTION

Only Fools and Horses is more than just a sitcom; it's a cultural phenomenon that has captured the hearts of millions around the world. Its enduring appeal lies in its perfect blend of comedy, relatable characters, and heartfelt storytelling, making it a timeless classic that continues to resonate with audiences of all ages. One of the biggest draws of the show is undoubtedly its memorable characters. Del Boy, the lovable but ambitious market trader, and his long suffering younger brother Rodney bring a delightful dynamic to the screen. Their banter, mishaps, and crackpot schemes provide endless laughter, making us feel like part of the Trotter family ourselves. Supporting characters such as Trigger, Boycie, Grandad, and Uncle Albert add to the show's charm, each contributing their own unique quirks that have become iconic in their own right.

This memorable world was all created by the much missed John Sullivan. 1000 Only Fools and Horses Facts, as the title implies!, offers no less than 1000 facts all about this legendary show.

1000 ONLY FOOLS AND HORSES FACTS

(1) The character of Del Boy clearly owes something to George Cole's Arthur Daley in the classic ITV show Minder - which began in 1979, two years before Only Fools and Horses.

Arthur Daley is a car salesman and businessman who is always up to his neck in trouble with his wheeling and dealing and dodgy deals in working-class London. Arthur is the sort of person who will get hold of some British Rail jam (which fell off the back of a lorry), change the labels, then try and flog it to hotels as a gourmet condiment.

When he was pitching Fools and Horses to the BBC, John Sullivan pointed out the popularity of Minder and said his show would have some similarities. Minder (which could be violent as Dennis Waterman's minder/bodyguard character Terry had a fight with some baddie most weeks) was obviously a drama rather than a sitcom but it was often very funny. You could argue too that the influences go both ways.

In its early days Minder was a vehicle for Dennis Waterman (who had just come off The Sweeney) but the role of Arthur Daley gradually became more pronounced to take advantage of George Cole's memorable comic performance. Minder's slant into a more comedic show with Arthur Daley front and centre may well have been inspired by the success the BBC were having with Fools and Horses and the Del Boy character. My advice is to simply watch both shows! Only Fools and Horses and Minder both remain classic comfort television.

(2) The abbreviation of Trotters Independent Traders is TIT. John Sullivan said this was not a deliberate joke because it never occurred to him at the time. The show did though play up this joke in the end - once John had noticed it.

(3) In the 1981 episode Go West Young Man, Del and Rodney get the numbers of two women in a nightclub. The young brunette woman named Michelle is played by Caroline Ellis. Caroline Ellis was cultish in the United States in her younger years for her role in The Bugaloos. The Bugaloos was a children's television series, produced by brothers Sidney Krofft and Martin Krofft, that aired on NBC on Saturday mornings from 1970 to 1972. The surreal psychedelic show features a musical group composed of four British teenagers who live in the fictional Tranquility Forest. They wear insect-themed outfits with antennae and wings which allow them to fly. The Bugaloos is fondly remembered by those who watched it as kids and the greatest moment in Bugaloos history was surely Caroline's character Joy singing The Senses of Our World. Caroline Ellis didn't do much acting after The Bugaloos so her appearance in Only Fools and Horses is something of a novelty and collector's item.

(4) In 1981, the year the first episode of Only Fools and Horses went out, Margaret Thatcher was the Prime Minister, Ronald Reagan became the President, Muhammad Ali fought for the last time, the Yorkshire Ripper was arrested, and Prince Charles and Lady Diana Spencer got married.

(5) In the first series of Fools and Horses there was

completely different titles music - a jaunty theme by the great Ronnie Hazlehurst. John Sullivan hated this theme and insisted on it being replaced in the second series and you can understand why if you listen to it. Not only is it a racket it also feels inappropriate for the show. Ronnie Hazlehurst did some wonderful themes but Fools and Horses was assuredly not one of them.

(6) The episode It Never Rains saw the characters go to Benidorm but the BBC didn't have the budget to shoot it abroad so they shot it in Dorset and just pretended the characters were in Spain. In the later years of the show they would go abroad for real to shoot episodes if the story required it but early on they simply didn't have the clout or money to do this.

(7) Trevor Francis is mentioned in the Only Fools and Horses closing song. Trevor Francis was the first footballer in England to cost a million pounds. He won 52 caps for England and scored the winning goal for Nottingham Forest in the 1979 European Cup Final.

(8) When it was first transmitted, the average audiences for Only Fools and Horses were about 7 million. Although viewing figures like that would be considered quite decent today, back in 1981 they were considered very poor (this was obviously a time when a LOT more people watched television - there were only three channels and no internet or streaming). As a consequence of this some (though not all) in the BBC were ambivalent about Fools and Horses getting a second series and could easily have axed the show.

(9) The name of Nelson Mandela House in the show was inspired by left-wing London councils of this era naming buildings after Nelson Mandela as a nose thumb to the

Margaret Thatcher government. The Thatcher government called Mandela a terrorist.

(10) David Jason said that at his audition for Only Fools and Horses someone at the BBC presumed he had come to read for the part of Grandad. This was obviously a consequence of the fact that David was previously aged up to play Blanco - the old lag in the classic prison sitcom Porridge. David's stock in trade in the past had often been playing comic characters much older than him.

(11) When they came back for the last three specials, John Sullivan said he decided to have Del Boy lose his money because a lot of the comedy and essence of the show would be lost if Del was wealthy. Having Del Boy swanning around in the South of France for three episodes drinking champagne wouldn't really feel like Only Fools and Horses.

(12) The full address of Del and Rodney is 368 Nelson Mandela House, Dockside Estate, Peckham.

(13) In the episode The Unlucky Winner Is, Rodney has to pretend to be fourteen after Del Boy (using one of Rodney's childhood paintings) wins a competition to go on holiday to Spain. Nicholas Lyndhurst was about 28 in real life when this episode was made so it probably isn't very realistic that he could pass for a fourteen year-old!

(14) It was the producer Ray Butt who saw the potential of Fools and Horses. Ray Butt would direct many episodes himself in the early series. Ray had worked on many famous sitcoms like Last of the Summer Wine and are You Being Served?

(15) The 1987 Christmas special The Frog's Legacy was the

last episode that Ray Butt directed before he left the show. Ray told John Sullivan that The Frog's Legacy should be the last ever episode because the show was past its sell by date. John Sullivan obviously disagreed with this but he did make some changes - putting more focus on the private lives of the Trotters. This proved a great success with viewers and the show became more of a comedy drama than a sitcom.

(16) According to media reports at the time, David Jason was paid £300,000 to appear in the last three Only Fools and Horses specials (broadcast from 2001). Adjusted for inflation, that would be over £600,000 in today's money.

(17) Chas & Dave were supposed to sing the Fools and Horses theme song but they were unavailable when it had to be recorded so John Sullivan did it instead. A lot of people (including me) grew up thinking that it was Nicholas Lyndhurst as Rodney singing the Fools and Horses theme song. It wasn't - though it does sound a lot like him.

(18) Only Fools and Horses was actually the name of an episode in John Sullivan's previous sitcom Citizen Smith. Citizen Smith ran between 1977 and 1980 and starred Robert Lindsay as a (comical) revolutionary in Tooting, London.

(19) The BBC went to great lengths to keep it secret that Del and Rodney would dress as Batman and Robin in the episode Heroes and Villains. The scene would be much funnier if it came as a surprise to the audience so it was important that it didn't get spoiled.

(20) Trigger's sole qualification is a Grade 3 Cycling Proficiency Diploma.

(21) John Challis said that Boycie's 'machine gun' style laugh was based on the laugh of a woman he used to know!

(22) The highest rated episode of Only Fools and Horses on IMDB is a tie between The Jolly Boys' Outing (1989) and Time on Our Hands (1996). Both of these episodes scored a stellar 9.6 out of 10.

(23) Tessa Peake-Jones had never actually watched any of Only Fools and Horses when she was cast as Raquel.

(24) A British Film Institute poll by industry experts in 2000 ranked Only Fools and Horses 45th in a poll of the 100 greatest ever British television shows.

(25) One of Del Boy's ambitions was to be a yuppie. Yupppie means "young upwardly-mobile professional". It was a phrase which entered the lexicon in the Thatcher era. Yuppies were generally considered to be pretentious and vain but Del seems blissfully unaware of this!

(26) Del Boy is partial to a Piña Colada. The piña colada is a cocktail made with rum, cream of coconut, and pineapple juice, usually served either blended or shaken with ice.

(27) Del Boy's famous three wheeled van is not a Robin Reliant but a Reliant Regal Supervan III. These vans were produced between 1963 and 1972.

(28) Del Boy later got a four-wheeled car - a Capri Ghia.

(29) In the episode Sickness And Wealth, Trigger mentions Jimmy Savile during the seance. It was actually a funny joke at the time but in light of later revelations this joke is understandably edited out of the episode now on repeats.

(30) Damien Trotter was portrayed by five different child actors in the show. Douglas Hodge also played the adult Damien in a nightmare sequence Rodney has.

(31) The early series of Fools and Horses were episodic and could be watched in any order. Later series though required the audience to be more aware of the lives of Del and Rodney and what had happened in previous episodes.

(32) The interiors in Del and Rodney's flat were filmed in a studio. For the exterior shots of the tower block (Nelson Mandela House in the show), Harlech Tower in Acton, West London was used from 1981 to 1985. Harlech Tower has been scheduled for demolition for quite a few years now. David Jason is among those who would like the tower to be preserved. Some of the real residents of this tower block don't seem to be quite so sentimental about it. Given a choice they'd rather live somewhere else.

(33) From 1988, Whitemead House in Ashton in Bristol took over as the exterior location for Nelson Mandela House in Fools and Horses. The odd thing about this change of exterior is that Whitemead House, with its dark orange bricks, looked very different to Harlech Tower. Presumably, they just hoped viewers wouldn't notice!

(34) Although the show is set in Peckham a lot of it was actually filmed in Bristol later on. The car park of Bristol City football club was used for some of the market scenes.

(35) Buster Merryfield's real name was Harry. He preferred to go by the name Buster - a nickname he'd had since childhood.

(36) David Jason's personal copy of the script for the

episode Heroes and Villains sold for £4,100 at a 2019 auction.

(37) Lennard Pearce was only in his sixties when he played Grandad in Only Fools and Horses. He actually looks a lot older.

(38) David Jason and Nicholas Lyndhurst look nothing like brothers but this became part of the show because it is implied that they might not share the same father. This did indeed turn out to be the case in the end.

(39) The early frontrunner for the part of Del Boy was Enn Reitel - who is fairly unknown today. Enn Reitel is a Scottish actor often associated with comic roles. He later supplied voices for Spitting Image and did a lot of voice acting for video games. Reitel had other commitments at the time which eventually ruled him out of contention for Only Fools and Horses.

(40) The Green Green Grass was a spin-off show in which the characters of Boycie and Marlene, along with son Tyler, move to a farm in Shropshire to lay low after Boycie gives evidence against the Driscoll Brothers. There were 32 episodes of The Green Green Grass between 2005 and 2009. Roy Marsden and Christopher Ryan made some guest appearances as Danny and Tony Driscoll. Paul Barber as Denzil also appeared in one episode. Aside from this there were no guest appearances from Fools and Horses actors. John Sullivan wrote some - but not all - episodes of The Green Green Grass.

(41) Though it was undemanding fun and had its fans, it is probably fair to say that The Green Green Grass is not considered to be a classic sitcom. It felt a bit broad and

unrealistic compared to Fools and Horses - most of the comedy coming from the culture clash between Boycie and some cartoonish country bumpkins.

(42) Eva Mottley played Denzil's wife Corrine in Only Fools and Horses but, tragically, she committed suicide in 1985 at the age of 31. Out of respect to Eva's memory, John Sullivan decided not to recast the part and so instead it was written into the show that Denzil got divorced.

(43) The BBC staggered the release of the last three Christmas specials (If They Could See Us Now, Strangers on the Shore, Sleepless in Peckham). Instead of showing them all over one Christmas they were each shown a year apart. This was probably a mistake because it hampered the flow of an ongoing story. The last special (in 2003) had several million less viewers than the first 2001 special so clearly a number of people had lost interest or completely forgotten the previous specials by then. It did seem a bit mean of the BBC to ration the release of these specials in that way. The general theory is that the BBC got 'greedy' and saw a means to dominate not one but THREE Christmas ratings battles!

(44) Strangers on the Shore was broadcast at 9:40pm by the BBC. This was a very odd timeslot for such a beloved family show. They probably lost some viewers by putting it on so late.

(45) The episode Strained Relations revolves around the funeral of Grandad (Lennard Pearce had sadly passed away in real life). It was unusual at the time for a sitcom to address the death of a late actor's character like this but John Sullivan was determined to do an episode which payed tribute to Grandad and Lennard Pearce. Last of the Summer Wine later did something similar when episodes dealt with

Compo's funeral after the death of Bill Owen.

(46) Nicholas Lyndhurst and David Jason both said they found it difficult to make the episode which dealt with Grandad's death because they had been very fond of Lennard Pearce. They said the mood on set was very bleak and sad when they shot that episode.

(47) At the time of his death, Lennard Pearce had just started shooting the episode Hole in One. John Sullivan had to quickly write Strained Relations to address Grandad's death in the show. Hole in One was then completed with Buster Merryfield replacing Lennard Pearce in the scenes that Lennard had shot.

(48) Rodney seems to find Damien a bit spooky. This is a comic riff based on Damien sharing a name with Damien Thorn. Damien Thorn is the antagonist of The Omen horror franchise. He is the Antichrist and the son of the Devil. It was actually Rodney who suggested naming the kid Damien but he was only joking!

(49) Raquel was only supposed to appear in one episode but John Sullivan liked the chemistry between David Jason and Tessa Peake-Jones so he brought the character back in the end and she became a regular.

(50) Only Fools and Horses got a prequel show in 2010 with Rock & Chips. Sadly though, only a pilot and two specials had been made when John Sullivan passed away and so the show ended. Rock & Chips is set during the early 1960s and revolves around Del Boy's mother Joan (Kellie Bright) and how she had an affair with a rogue named Freddie "the Frog" Robdal (played by Nicholas Lyndhurst - who featured in a photograph as Freddie at the end of Only

Fools and Horses) - which spawned Rodney. Joan is obviously never seen in Only Fools and Horses because she died before that show's timeline began so John Sullivan thought it would be interesting for us to see what Joan was like. The teenage Del Boy is played by Inbetweeners actor James Buckley. We also meet young versions of Boycie, Denzil, Trigger, and Roy Slater. Phil Daniels plays Grandad while Shaun Dingwall is the lazy Reg Trotter. John Sullivan came up with the idea for Rock & Chips in 1996 but it went on the backburner for a long time due to The Green Green Grass going into production.

Rock & Chips seems to be slightly forgotten these days - which is perhaps a consequence of the fact that so few episodes (or specials in this case) were made. The reviews from critics were middling but audiences and fans seemed to quite like the show.

(51) It is sometimes said that Tessa Peake-Jones was in the first ever episode of Fools and Horses as an extra. John Sullivan apparently debunked this though as an urban myth.

(52) The production of Only Fools and Horses had three Reliant Regals. One was used as the main vehicle and there were two identical back-up vans in case something went wrong with the main one.

(53) An early choice to play Del Boy was Jim Broadbent. However, Jim Broadbent was unavailable due to stage commitments and didn't want the part anyway. He would obviously later make three appearances in the show as another character - the corrupt copper Roy Slater.

(54) Jim Broadbent later said that it was for the best that he

didn't take the part of Del Boy in Only Fools and Horses because he wouldn't have wanted to be stuck in one show for very long and probably would have left after two or three series.

(55) One of Del Boy's favourite sayings is - "He who dares, wins!" This was clearly inspired by the SAS motto.

(56) The Driscoll Brothers only appeared in one episode of Fools and Horses. Played by Roy Marsden and Christopher Ryan, these gangsters don't look like brothers at all - which makes them like Del and Rodney. The Driscolls are greatly feared on the Peckham manor and not to be crossed.

(57) Three pubs in Bristol - The White Horse in Bedminster, the Bristol Flyer on Gloucester Road, and the Waggon and Horses - were later used as exterior shooting locations for The Nag's Head pub in Fools and Horses.

(58) Another actor who was considered for the part of Del Boy before David Jason was Billy Murray. Billy Murray has been in many, many things but is probably best known for his part as Johnny Allen in EastEnders. He seems to make a lot of British gangster films these days. Ray Butt went to see Billy Murray in a play but judged him wrong for the part of Del Boy. It wasn't a wasted trip though because Roger Lloyd-Pack was also in the play. Ray Butt liked Roger so much he cast him as Trigger.

(59) We see Del Boy and some other characters use early mobile phones in the show. The first mobile phones were the size of bricks and had terrible reception.

(60) The rings and jewelry that David Jason wore in the show as Del Boy was all fake in reality.

(61) Trigger wasn't quite as dim in the early episodes. Having a character who is not very bright is a common sitcom trope but Trigger, in the hands of Roger Lloyd-Pack, is surely one of the greatest examples of this trope. You get the impression that everything Trigger says, no matter how daft, has perfect logic to him!

(62) Grandad's full name is Edward Kitchener "Ted" Trotter.

(63) Rodney calls Del's Capri 'the Pratmobile'.

(64) Del considered giving Damien the name Troy and Raquel suggested Aron. They obviously went with Rodney's (flippant) suggestion of Damien in the end.

(65) Apparently, John Sullivan was writing a new Fools and Horses special circa 2010/2011 and David Jason was open to the idea of returning as Del Boy. John Sullivan's sad death in 2011 ended this possibility.

(66) Del Boy was supposed to have permed hair but David Jason vetoed this idea.

(67) On a 1998 VHS release, the two Miami Twice episodes were released as one single long movie.

(68) Boycie's real name is Herman Aubrey Boyce.

(69) James Buckley said that when he played the young Del Boy in Rock & Chips it was agreed that he shouldn't try to impersonate David Jason. This was a teenage Del Boy so he wasn't going to be the same person as the older Del Boy we see in Only Fools and Horses. James said that he had lunch with David Jason when he got the part and this was a great

honour.

(70) Uncle Albert's middle name is Gladstone.

(71) Paul Barber played Denzil in eighteen episodes of Fools and Horses. Denzil is from Liverpool but moved to London when he was 13. Denzil is an old friend of Del Boy and works as a lorry driver.

(72) Kenneth MacDonald played the pub landlord Mike in Fools and Horses. Kenneth sadly died in 2001. When they made the last three specials Mike's absence was explained by him being prison for embezzling money.

(73) Sidney "Sid" Robertson (played by Roy Heather) ran the unhygienic cafe in Fools and Horses. In the last three specials we see that Sid is running the pub for the absent Mike. Sid's Cafe is another element that connects Only Fools and Horses to Minder because in the latter show Terry McCann would often visit a grotty cafe where the lack of hygiene and terrible food was used for comic effect.

(74) In the prequel show Rock & Chips, we learn that Rodney was named after the Australian actor Rod Taylor after Joan watched the classic sci-fi film The Time Machine.

(75) John Sullivan's favourite episode of Fools and Horses was the 1988 Christmas special Dates.

(76) Del Boy rarely - if ever - seems to pay any tax. This is a trait he shares with Arthur Daley.

(77) A Touch of Glass has one of the most famous Fools and Horses scenes when the Trotters break an expensive Chandelier by loosening the wrong one. Nicholas Lyndhurst

said they had to do this in one take because it would be too costly to shoot again. The cast and crew were ordered not to laugh while this scene was shot.

(78) A YouGov poll in 2015 had Only Fools and Horses comfortably at number one when it came to Britain's greatest sitcom.

(79) John Sullivan and David Jason both disliked the episode A Royal Flush and wish they hadn't made it. In this episode Rodney has a chance of romance with high society beauty Lady Victoria but Del Boy ruins everything with his obnoxious behaviour. Del Boy comes across as mean-spirited and cruel in A Royal Flush - and this is definitely out of character with the Del Boy we know and love. John Sullivan insisted this episode be edited for DVD release so that Del Boy came off as less obnoxious.

(80) Rodney functions as the 'everyman' character in Fools and Horses. We relate to Rodney because he is (most of the time anyway) more realistic and level headed than Del Boy.

(81) David Jason wrote in his memoir that the one thing television and film industry people were always in awe of was the way he was able to eat and act at the same time during a scene - which is not an easy thing to do! Ever notice how in films and TV shows people are often served some food and then never eat it? By contrast, Del Boy and David's Jack Frost character in A Touch of Frost are both frequently munching on food during scenes.

(82) John Sullivan based the Driscoll Brothers on the Richardson Brothers. The Richardson brothers, Charlie and Eddie, were notorious figures in London's criminal underworld during the 1960s.

(83) Rock & Chips features a 'Jolly Boys' outing to Margate so this was clearly a tradition Del and his friends kept going for a long time.

(84) Nicholas Lyndhurst was the first person to be cast in Fools and Horses. John Sullivan had some doubts about Nicholas playing Rodney because he though Nicholas was a bit too middle-class for the part. However, Nicholas aced the audition and showed he was perfectly capable of convincingly playing a working-class character - something he'd already done anyway in the Porridge spin-off Going Straight.

(85) Del Boy has a little mini-bar in the corner of his flat. This is considered to be a bit naff these days but it was by no means uncommon in the 70s and 80s.

(86) For the sixth series in 1988, John Sullivan requested a budget increase and longer running times. The BBC agreed to both of these requests because Fools and Horses was one of their biggest shows. It is said the budget for the increased by 40% from series six onwards.

(87) Buster Merryfield said it was terrifying shooting in front of a live studio audience when he joined Only Fools and Horses.

(88) The old phrase 'only fools and horses work for a living' inspired the title of the show.

(89) Trigger seems to think Rodney's name is Dave. The initial explanation was supposed to be that Trigger was pretending not to know Rodney's name to belittle him but this was changed to Trigger genuinely NOT knowing Rodney wasn't called Dave.

(90) According to the late John Challis, Anthony Hopkins loved Only Fools and Horses and was supposed to make a guest appearance as one of the Driscoll brothers. However, there was a schedule clash with Silence of the Lambs so he had to be replaced.

(91) Only Fools and Horses implies that it might be doubtful if Tyler is Boycie's biological son because Boycie has a low sperm count and Marlene seems a bit over familiar with Del Boy and other men on the manor.

(92) In the early episodes Trigger is supposed to be a small time criminal. They moved away from this though and made him a road sweeper.

(93) Patrick Murray appeared in 20 episodes of Fools and Horses as Rodney's friend Mickey Pearce. Mickey was a bit of a spiv and ducker and diver and not someone you would want to place too much trust in. Mickey was sort of a vague prototype for Jay in The Inbetweeners in that he was prone to embellish and exaggerate his romantic and business escapades.

(94) 24 million people in Britain watched the 1996 episode Time on Our Hands when it first broadcast. Viewing figures like that for a sitcom would be impossible today. At the time it was presumed this would be the last ever episode.

(95) David Jason planned to leave Only Fools and Horses after the fifth series to do other acting work. In the end he changed his mind and stayed with the show. If he had left the BBC's plan in this scenario was to make a spin-off show with Rodney as the main character. John Sullivan had actually started writing the spin-off show - which had the working title Hot Rod.

(96) If David Jason had left the show after series five his departure would obviously have been explained by him accepting Jumbo Mills' offer to go to Australia. When David decided to stay with the show it was changed so that Del declined Jumbo's offer.

(97) There were 64 episodes of Only Fools and Horses.

(98) Del's mother died in 1964 and his father Reg left soon after. This meant that Del Boy had to look after both Rodney and Grandad from a young age. Del Boy frequently reminds Rodney of this in the show.

(99) A UK Gold poll in 2022 voted Del falling through the bar as the funniest ever sitcom moment.

(100) Fools and Horses lore is slightly inconsistent on Rodney and Del's age gap but it is generally listed as thirteen years. This is contradicted though more than a few times. In real life, David Jason is 21 years older than Nicholas Lyndhurst.

(101) David Jason was briefly cast as Corporal Jones in Dad's Army but at the last minute the BBC decided they wanted Clive Dunn instead.

(102) Grandad usually has two televisions playing simultaneously. Saves having to change channels!

(103) The show's closing song is called Hooky Street. Hooky is a slang word for something that fell off the back of a lorry. In other words, it was pilfered!

(104) What makes the Batman & Robin scene in Heroes and Villains even funnier is that they are wearing the costumes

from the old Adam West television show and we hear music cues from that show too. Notice how Rodney punches his palm in frustration just like Burt Ward as Robin used to do.

(105) One of the Reliant Regal vans used in the show sold for £44,000 in 2007.

(106) John Sullivan said it was always his plan that the Trotters would be millionaires near the end of the show.

(107) Steven Woodcock played Jevon in five episodes of Fools and Horses in 1988-1989. The reason he didn't become a regular is that Steven took the part of Clyde Tavernier in EastEnders in 1990. Steven appeared in 201 episodes of EastEnders so it was impossible for him to do Fools and Horses at the same time.

(108) James Buckley said that in preparation for his role as Del Boy in the prequel Rock & Chips, he binged all 64 episodes of Only Fools and Horses!

(109) Rock & Chips was more of a drama than a sitcom. It wasn't shot in front of a studio audience like the base show.

(110) Before he died, John Sullivan had plans for Rock & Chips to move away from Joan and Freddie and focus more on Del Boy and Grandad.

(111) The biggest grossing film of 1981, the year the first episode of Only Fools and Horses went out, was Raiders of the Lost Ark.

(112) John Sullivan said that when he first started writing Fools and Horses the BBC complained about the cockney rhyming slang and working-class vernacular of the

characters!

(113) In a Radio Times poll in 2009, a panel of 'comedy experts' ranked Only Fools and Horses as the sixth greatest British sitcom of all time. Fawlty Towers topped the poll.

(114) Del and Rodney made a visually mismatched pair of brothers because David Jason is 5'5 and Nicholas Lyndhurst is 6'1.

(115) The episode Yuppy Love has the most famous Fools and Horses moment of all when Del Boy falls through the bar at the wine bar. John Sullivan said this was based on a real incident because he had once witnessed someone do a similar thing at a bar.

(116) David Jason and Nicholas Lyndhurst accepted a lifetime achievement gong at the National Film Awards in 2017.

(117) A Only Fools and Horses stage musical for the West End was launched in 2019. Paul Whitehouse, who also supplied lyrics, played Grandad. The cast had Tom Bennett as Del and Ryan Hutton as Rodney. The musical condenses the entire Fools and Horses history into a two hour show. Paul Whitehouse wrote the show with John Sullivan's son Jim.

(118) David Jason said in an interview that Del Boy isn't a crook or criminal but someone who 'bends the rules' to eke out a living. Del Boy might not always be honest or on the right side of the law but he's essentially a decent man who means well.

(119) The big ring Del Boy wears in the show only cost 50p

in real life.

(120) Robin Nedwell was considered for the part of Del Boy. Nedwell was best known for his role in the sitcom Doctor in the House.

(121) David Jason had a lot of input into the clothes Del Boy wore in the show.

(122) In the episode Mother Nature's Son, Del Boy has the idea of selling tap water as Peckham Spring water.

In 2004, the Coca-Cola Company launched their bottled water brand Dasani in Britain. The press found out that Dasani was actually tap water from Sidcup which had been treated and put in fancy bottles. Coca-Cola removed the Dasani brand from Britain after this story broke. As you might imagine, a lot of the coverage of this story noted the similarity between what Del Boy and Coca-Cola did. In this case, life imitated art!

(123) John Sullivan was not initially convinced that David Jason should play Del Boy. He felt David was too associated with wimpy browbeaten characters like Granville (from Open All Hours) and Blanco from Porridge.

(124) The 2001 Christmas special of Only Fools and Horses was the most watched single television show of that decade with an incredible 74% audience share.

(125) David Jason said he has a soft spot for the episode Diamonds Are For Heather - though some fans tend to find this one of the weaker episodes. Diamonds Are For Heather is an interesting episode because it is one of the first stories in the show which balances drama and comedy in equal

measure.

(126) The famous Channel 4 sitcom Desmond's (which ran from 1989 to 1994) was - like Fools and Horses - set in Peckham. I like to think they take place in the same universe and the characters from both shows know each other.

(127) Among Del's most common insults are to call someone (usually Rodney) a 'plonker' or a 'dipstick'.

(128) John Sullivan's son Jim, who wrote episodes of The Green Green Grass, considered writing new episodes of Rock & Chips after his father died but in the end he decided it probably wouldn't be a good idea.

(129) David Jason said it was so much fun making Only Fools and Horses that it never felt like work to him.

(130) The 1985 Christmas special To Hull And Back did some location shooting in Amsterdam.

(131) The medal that Trigger got in the show for services to road sweeping sold for £4,900 at a 2019 auction.

(132) David Jason said that him and Nicholas Lyndhurst found it difficult to keep a straight face when they wore their Batman and Robin costumes shooting Heroes and Villains.

(133) John Sullivan deliberately chose to have a large age gap between Del and Rodney because there was a large age gap between him and his sister.

(134) It was reported in 2010 that repeats of Only Fools

and Horses had resulted in a tourism boom for Peckham!

(135) It is claimed that you have to pay the BBC a couple of thousand pounds in order to show the Del falling through the bar clip on television.

(136) There were reports in the media in 2013 that David Jason was mulling over a new Fools and Horses script written by John Sullivan's sons and based on notes their father had left. Nothing came of this though and no new episode was made. Fake news?

(137) Del Boy's full name is Derek Edward Trotter.

(138) There was a special Only Fools and Horses ten minute short film for Sports Relief in 2014 called Beckham in Peckham. David Beckham guest starred with David Jason and Nicholas Lyndhurst in the sketch. David and Nicholas slip back into the characters of Del and Rodney in Beckham in Peckham as if they've never been away.

(139) Carry On legend Joan Sims played Trigger's aunt (Reenie) in the Christmas special The Frog's Legacy. The character was played by Emma Cooke in the prequel show Rock & Chips.

(140) David Jason said it was David Beckham who suggested doing a Fools and Horses sketch for Sports Relief. Beckham was a big fan of the show.

(141) One of Del's most common catchphrases is "This time next year, we'll be millionaires!" He was eventually right about that!

(142) Del Boy mentions The Onedin line in To Hull and

Back. This is a joke based on the fact that Philip Bond (who plays Van Kleefe in To Hull and Back) was in The Onedin Line. The Onedin Line was an early 1970s BBC seafaring drama set in 19th century Liverpool.

(143) The Sports Relief charity night in 2014 got an average of 7 million viewers. However, that spiked to 9 million when the Only Fools and Horses sketch was shown.

(144) David Jason said the second part of Miami Twice was one of his favourite episodes of Fools and Horses because he got to play two characters - Del Boy and mafia boss Vincenzo "Vinny the Chain" Occhetti. I'm not sure many fans would rank this as one of their favourite episodes!

(145) The Beckham in Peckham special for Sports Relief took two days to film. It was shot at Wimbledon Studios.

(146) John Sullivan said that Rodney's personality was based on himself at that age. John said he was a bit of a dreamer - a quality we see in Rodney.

(147) Only Fools and Horses has more 'merch' traded on eBay than any other British sitcom.

(149) When it comes to football, it seems that Rodney is a Chelsea fan.

(150) The lowest rated episode of Only Fools and Horses on IMDB is (no surprise here) A Royal Flush. Its rating of 7.1 is still pretty decent though by most standards.

(151) Buster Merryfield was a schoolboy and army boxing champion.

(152) 'Mental Mickey' in the episode It's Only Rock and Roll gets very annoyed when anyone suggests he was ever in Rampton. Rampton Secure Hospital is a high-security psychiatric hospital. This is one of the places they tend to send insane serial killers.

(153) 'Mental Mickey' might not have been in Rampton but he suggests he was at Broadmoor. Broadmoor Hospital is ANOTHER place they tend to send serial killers.

(154) Sue Holderness said she had a close encounter with an alligator while shooting the Miami Twice episode in Florida!

(155) Although Uncle Albert enjoys a drop of rum in the show, Buster Merryfield was teetotal in real life.

(156) Uncle Albert's War Medal sold for £4,700 at a 2021 auction.

(157) David Jason has said, and he makes a good point, that Del Boy driving the battered Reliant makes no sense because Del Boy is all about image and trying to appear sophisticated and successful. Wouldn't a man like Del Boy get a flash car - like how Arthur Daley always drives a Jag in Minder to project an image of status and success? Maybe we can just presume that Del Boy has a sentimental attachment to the van?

(158) Rodney has two GCEs. The GCE was replaced in 1988 by the GCSE. Both of these qualification are basically the level before A'Levels.

(159) The series five episode The Longest Night may have been influenced by Minder as the first ever episode of

Minder also revolved around a hostage situation in a supermarket.

(160) Roger Lloyd-Pack said that when he was out and about in public, people would often shout "Trigger!" when they saw him! Roger said this could be a bit annoying.

(161) Nicholas Lyndhurst said in a 2013 interview that Only Fools and Horses would never be commissioned these days because television companies are more interested in trashy talent shows than developing quality sitcoms.

(162) There was big ratings battle at Christmas 1985 when The Fools and Horses Christmas special To Hull and Back went out at the same time as the feature length Minder special Minder On the Orient Express. In the end the BBC won the battle over ITV as Fools and Horses got a few more million viewers than Minder On the Orient Express.

(163) David Jason said he loved Minder and never considered that show and Fools and Horses to be rivals.

(164) The Only Fools and Horses musical was something that John Sullivan had been working on when he sadly died.

(165) Del Boy is partial to a curry - or Ruby Murray as he might say.

(166) David Jason received a knighthood in 2005 for his services to acting.

(167) Del Boy is fond of using French phrases - which of course he always gets hopelessly wrong. Del is the sort of person who will say "Au revoir" when he meets someone!

(168) Nicholas Lyndhurst said they sometimes felt under pressure on Fools and Horses because they knew that millions of people would be watching and the show had to live up to expectations.

(169) Richard Branson has a cameo in the first part of Miami Twice. He is a terrible actor!

(170) It was reported in 2022 that a fan of the show named Danny Burge had named all eight of his dogs after characters from Only Fools and Horses.

(171) In the episode Video Nasty, Del Boy comes up with a plot for Rodney's proposed film - a rhino gets loose in a city! It seems possible that this might have derived from John Sullivan being familiar with a 1974 comedy film with Gene Wilder and Zero Mostel called Rhinoceros. In the film, people in a city start turning into rhinoceroses - leading to much comic chaos. This film didn't do very well and has, despite its cast, been almost completely forgotten.

(172) Buster Merryfield was not exactly posh but definitely a bit more well spoken than Uncle Albert. That obviously wasn't his real accent in the show. Lennard Pearce was also a bit posher sounding in real life than Grandad in the show.

(173) For the supermarket in The Longest Night, a real Co-op supermarket in Leytonstone, East London was used for the exteriors and some (but not all) of the interiors. This supermarket was apparently closed years ago and is now a completely different store.

(174) The Bee Gees singer Barry Gibb made a cameo in Miami Twice. Barry was such a big fan of Fools and Horses he had tapes of the show sent to him in America.

(175) The 1985 Christmas special To Hull And Back was one of only two episodes shot on film rather than video. The other episode shot on film was Miami Twice – Part Two.

(176) Del and Rodney not having the same father was first hinted at in the 1983 episode Thicker than Water.

(177) Tony Anholt played Abdul in To Hull and Back. Tony Anholt did many things but is probably best known for his role as Charles Frere in the late 1980s Sunday night yacht themed soap/drama Howard's Way. I always remember Tony as Tony Verdeschi in Space: 1999.

(178) Although the character Reg Trotter (Del's father) features in Rock & Chips, Reg only made one appearance in Only Fools and Horses. This was the 1983 episode Thicker than Water. Reg was played by Peter Woodthorpe. Peter Woodthorpe was cast because he did bear a certain resemblance to David Jason. Trivia you will never need - Peter Woodthorpe was the voice of Pigsy in the dubbed version of the cult Japanese action show Monkey. British kids in the early 1980s used to watch Monkey on Friday teatime.

(179) The brand of cigars that Del Boy smokes is, according to a comment by his doctor in one episode, Castella. David Jason actually did some commercials for this brand. Del Boy's love of cigars is something he shares with Arthur Daley.

(180) The episode Friday the 14th is a pun derived from the famous slasher film Friday the 13th.

(181) Nicholas Lyndhurst said he turned down a part in the famous film The Full Monty because it wasn't his cup of tea.

His Fools and Horses co-star Paul (Denzil) Barber did take a part in the film though.

(182) Sleepless in Peckham is a pun based on the Tom Hanks film Sleepless in Seattle.

(183) The film that Uncle Albert is watching in To Hull and Back is The Cruel Sea. The Cruel Sea is a 1953 British war film based on the novel of the same title by Nicholas Monsarrat. Jack Hawkins was the main star.

(184) Tessa Peake-Jones said the cast in the show have done very well from the fact Fools and Horses has been repeated so many times. They get a royalty cheque for the repeats.

(185) Rodney is usually deployed as a lookout when Del Boy is doing his market pitches.

(186) David Jason said, although the characters are supposed to be in Spain, it was absolutely freezing in Dorset when they shot the episode It Never Rains.

(187) Cash and Curry and The Longest Night are the only two episodes where we don't see the Trotter's flat.

(188) In 2022, a fan paid £6,000 at auction for a prop bottle of Peckham Spring Water signed by David Jason.

(189) In the episode Sleepless in Peckham, we learn that the coach company banned running 'Jolly Boys' outings to Margate after Del and his friends blew one of their coaches up!

(190) Cuts had to be made to some the Fools and Horses

DVD releases due to the BBC being unable to get the rights for some of the background music heard in the show.

(191) There was an Only Fools and Horses sketch at the 1986 Royal Variety performance featuring David Jason, Nicholas Lyndhurst, and Buster Merryfield.

(192) Tessa Peake-Jones made her first appearance as Raquel Turner in the 1988 Christmas episode Dates.

(193) A fair few people have made a living as a Del Boy lookalike. Many of them look nothing like David Jason!

(194) Jim Sullivan did a Where's Del Boy? children's book in 2023. The blurb went like this - 'National treasure hunt Fromage Frais! Del Boy Trotter is on the run, with dodgy detective Roy Slater hot on his heels. With the manhunt going from Peckham to Hull and from Margate to Miami, will the long arm of the law finally catch up with him? The police chase plays out over ten minutely detailed, search-and-find artworks, with Peckham Echo front pages, articles and adverts also dropped in throughout, to move the story along.

In this immersive plunge into the world of Only Fools and Horses, finding Del Boy is just the beginning. The pages are packed with artful clues, in-jokes and subtle references to all 64 episodes, testing the sleuthing skills of life-long fans of the classic show. Can Del Boy dodge the detective? Mange tout!'

(195) David Jason did not go to drama school. He left school at fifteen and worked in a garage.

(196) The Driscoll Brothers are first mentioned in the

episode Video Nasty.

(197) Del Boy often wears a flat cap. The flat cap used to be associated with the working-class but has long since been hijacked by hipsters and celebrities.

(198) Only Fools and Horses received a posthumous BAFTA Fellowship award for its creator, John Sullivan, in 2012.

(199) The show's popularity led to a 2019 Royal Mail stamp collection featuring the characters and iconic moments from Only Fools and Horses.

(200) The characters Mike and Denzil made their first appearance in Who's a Pretty Boy?

(201) Del Boy often refers to Rodney as 'bruv'.

(202) According to YouGov polling in Britain, David Jason is the 10th most popular actor. Morgan Freeman topped the poll.

(203) John Sullivan felt the second series was better than the first because he'd had six episodes to watch David Jason and Nicholas Lyndhurst and now had a much better grasp of how to write for these two actors.

(204) When the first episodes of Only Fools and Horses went out in 1981 the reviews from critics were middling at best. No one at the time could have possibly predicted that this would go on to become the most successful and beloved British sitcom of all time.

(205) After the first series of Fools and Horses ended, the BBC were in no rush to make a second series. At this point

in time they were struggling to see much potential or appeal in the show.

(206) In the episode Watching The Girls Go By, Albert mentions that his wartime flame Helga had a missing finger and Del asks if she got the finger caught in the til. This is a little nod to David Jason and Ronnie Barker's show Open All Hours - where the til in Arkwright's shop would slam of its own accord.

(207) Rodney's combat jacket in the early episodes was an item of clothing they found in the BBC costume department.

(208) Albert served (among other places) on the Russian Convoys. These were ships which sailed through Arctic conditions to deliver Allied aid to the Soviet Union to help them in their battle with Nazi Germany.

(209) The Frog's Legacy was more or less the start of the show moving away from half hour episodes to a longer format.

(210) In the episode The Class of 62, Trigger suggests the mystery person who has gathered them together might be Jeremy Beadle. Jeremy Beadle was famous for doing 'prank' shows in the 80s and 90s. He was on Game for a Laugh and then hosted Beadle's About.

(211) Nicholas Courtney appears in the episode Dates. His most famous role was as Brigadier Lethbridge-Stewart in Doctor Who. In tribute perhaps, Raquel says in Dates she once had a line in an episode of Doctor Who. Some years later Tessa Peake-Jones would appear in Doctor Who in the episode The Time of the Doctor.

(212) The swimming pool scenes in It Never Rains were shot at the Knoll House Hotel in Dorset.

(213) David Jason obviously had a crash mat for the scene in Yuppy Love where Del Boy falls through the bar. He would have been seriously injured otherwise!

(214) There were vague plans at one point to release The Jolly Boy's Outing as a theatrical film in cinemas. Palace Pictures were interested and the BBC liked the idea. It would have necessitated the running time being expanded somewhat. In the end though nothing came of this and it was shown on television.

(215) A salient reason why a lot of the show was shot in Bristol in the end is that it was too expensive to shoot in London. The show was never shot in Peckham but they did shoot some scenes in other parts of London. The producers didn't like shooting the show in London because it attracted too many interested onlookers - who could obviously be a pain if you are trying to shoot a scene and have limited time and money to get that scene in the can.

(216) A difference between Del Boy and Arthur Daley is that David Jason admired Del Boy and thought he was a decent man whereas George Cole saw Arthur Daley as an awful man and was horrified whenever anyone said they liked Arthur as a person.

(217) Del Boy has been known to order a Singapore sling. This cocktail contains lemon juice, dry gin, and cherry brandy.

(218) Rodney often wore a Dan Dare t-shirt early in the show. Dan Dare is a British science fiction comic hero who

appeared in the Eagle comic. Dan Dare was also in 2000 AD. The character was an ace pilot in the future - sort of like a mix of Biggles and Buck Rogers.

(219) Cassandra's full name is Cassandra Parry. In the end it was Cassandra Trotter.

(220) David Jason was 41 years-old when Only Fools and Horses began.

(221) Del Boy has ordered a Manhattan cocktail. This is made of whiskey, sweet vermouth, bitters, and a maraschino cherry garnish.

(222) John Sullivan said that one of the reasons why he wanted to do Only Fools and Horses is that he felt sitcoms had become too old-fashioned and were too often festooned with posh people. He wanted to do a working-class sitcom which felt more modern. He wanted East End boozers and tower blocks rather than stately homes and suburbia.

(223) By the time the fourth series aired, the viewing figures for Fools and Horses were double what they got in the first series.

(224) Only Fools and Horses was named the best sitcom of all time by the Heritage Foundation in 2001.

(225) John Sullivan said the comedy writers he loved the most were Ray Galton and Alan Simpson (who did Steptoe & Son and Hancock's Half Hour) and the American writer Neil Simon. Neil Simon wrote (among a great many other things) The Odd Couple and The Sunshine Boys.

(226) David Jason said that because his background was

sketch shows, sitcoms, and stage farces, there was a tendency to assume he couldn't act and was simply a comedian. The character of Del Boy gave David the chance to finally show what a great actor he was.

(227) A Slovenian re-make of fools and Horses was called Brat bratu (Brother to Brother). This only lasted for thirteen episodes.

(228) Del owns a Vauxhall Velox car early in the show. Del has to sell this car in Cash and Curry.

(229) Del's Reliant van has 'Trotters Independent Trading Co - New York – Paris – Peckham' written on the side!

(230) Boycie has a Jaguar E Type car.

(231) One of Del Boy's favourite meals is Duck à l'Orange.

(232) John Sullivan said that in his Fools and Horses scripts he would often write the direction 'cut to Rodney' because he knew that Nicholas Lyndhurst would then get a laugh with just a reaction or expression.

(233) The BBC got some letters of complaint about Danger UXD - the inflatable sex doll episode. Some parents said they didn't think this episode was suitable for the kids who watched the show each week.

(234) The inflatable dolls in Danger UXD were purchased in a Soho adult shop and then heavily modified to make them look less risque.

(235) John Sullivan said that when Only Fools and Horses first started he didn't think it would even get a second

series let alone go on to become a national institution.

(236) The beach scenes in It Never Rains were shot at Studland Beach, Dorset.

(237) John Sullivan said the only thing he would rather have been than a writer is a footballer.

(238) Paul Barber said he was genuinely terrified shooting the scene in The Jolly Boy's outing where Denzil goes on the pirate ship ride in the amusement park Dreamland.

(239) A 1969 Reliant Supervan was used in series one and two of Fools and Horses. Other models (from the early 1970s) were used later.

(240) Reliant was a British company who produced their cars in Tamworth.

(241) Del Boy has a cigar lighter shaped like a handgun.

(242) The Reliant Regal Supervan III had a top speed of 70 mph.

(243) When Fools and Horses first went out in 1981, it was up against ITV's The Flame Trees of Thika - a period miniseries with Hayley Mills. The Flame Trees of Thika won the ratings battle against Fools and Horses but who remembers The Flame Trees of Thika today?

(244) In a 2008 interview, John Sullivan said there would definitely be no more new episodes of Only Fools and Horses. It was a question he got asked a lot.

(245) John Sullivan (among other jobs) worked as a scene

shifter in television before he became a full time writer. Among the shows he 'shifted' scenery on were Porridge and To the Manor Born.

(246) Wanda Bentham, who played Cassandra's mother Pam, is the mother of the actor Benedict Cumberbatch.

(247) The show had a fairly small cast when it began. Aside from the main trio there was only really Trigger and Boycie.

(248) Del's yuppie suits in series six cost £200 each.

(249) David Jason was cast as Del Boy only weeks before filming was due to begin. They cut it very fine.

(250) Hooky Street is the name of the song used over the end titles. The opening credits song is called Only Fools and Horses.

(251) John Sullivan said he was very frustrated when the show's viewing figures remained disappointing in the first two series. He felt as if the show was invisible and no one even knew it existed.

(252) An eight-minute episode of Fools and Horses aired on 27 December 1982 as part of a show hosted by Frank Muir called The Funny Side of Christmas.

(253) When they become millionaires, Rodney buys Del Boy a Rolls Royce. The number plate reads - DEL 1.

(254) Rock & Chips was commissioned in 2003 but it only went into production in 2009.

(255) In the episode Rodney Comes Home, in reference to

AIDs, Del Boy says 'one wrong move and you could be shaking hands with Princess Di'. This was a reference to Princess Diana visiting AIDs patients in hospital. This line tends to be edited out of repeats.

(256) Shaun Dingwall, who played Reg Trotter in Rock & Chips, played the father of Billie Piper's character Rose in Doctor Who.

(257) Del is fond using the word 'brill' - which is obviously short for brilliant.

(258) The producer Gareth Gwenlan said there was enough material to make two series of Rock & Chips. Sadly though John Sullivan died only days after the last special went out.

(259) The Sky's the Limit (the satellite dish episode) was dropped from the repeat schedule for a time after the 9/11 attacks in New York due to the shot of the plane heading for the tower block.

(260) In 1976, David Jason was in an ITV sitcom called Lucky Fella about two plumber brothers who live in South East London. The show is interesting in that it has some similarities with Fools and Horses when it comes to the premise. The big difference is that David Jason is playing the more sensitive less domineering brother - which definitely wasn't the case with Only Fools and Horses.

(261) Del Boy and Jack Frost (David Jason's character in A Touch of Frost) both have the same middle name - Edward.

(262) Ray Butt floated the idea of doing an Only Fools and Horses stage show in the 1980s but John Sullivan was lukewarm about this idea so it never happened.

(263) Nicholas Lyndhurst said that A Touch of Glass might be his favourite episode.

(264) The episode The Unlucky Winner Is was written so it could be shot entirely in a studio. The reason for this is that everyone had a miserable time doing the location shooting in parky weather for It Never Rains - where they pretended Bournemouth was Spain.

(265) The last three Fools and Horses specials got some dreadful reviews in the newspapers. Many critics felt the specials were disappointing and that the show should have ended in 1996.

(266) Patrick Murray, who plays Mickey Pearce, had an injured arm when the episode Little Problems was shot. John Sullivan wrote this into the script - so the cast on his arm is explained by a beating from the Driscoll Brothers (or their goons at any rate).

(267) The episode title Rodney Come Home is a pun on the film Lassie Come Home.

(268) Although the Porridge spin-off show Going Straight, where Nicholas Lyndhurst played the teenage son of Ronnie Barker's Fletcher, was what helped persuade John sullivan Nicholas was right for the part of Rodney it must have been tricky to judge because Nicholas only has about four lines in Going Straight! Going Straight had Fletcher leaving prison and going home - where his wife has left him and his daughter is in a relationship with Fletch's old cellmate Lennie Godber (Richard Beckinsale). Going Straight was a really good show but it is largely forgotten today because it only ran to six episodes. The tragic death of Richard Beckinsale was the reason it ended.

(269) Del Boy and Arthur Daley both prefer cash to cheques - or Gregory's as they might say. Gregory Peck - cheque. In the company they keep you never know if a cheque will bounce.

(270) David Jason said if acting hadn't worked out for him he probably would have become a builder.

(271) Three Men, a Woman, and a Baby was the last 'regular' episode of Fools and Horses. After this there were only specials.

(272) If, as originally planned, David Jason had left Fools and Horses after the fifth series we would never have got to see Del Boy falling through the bar!

(273) Del Boy makes reference to 'Maxwell pension money' in the first part of Miami Twice. Robert Maxwell was a wealthy and famous British publishing magnate who was found to have secretly (and illegally) raided the pension funds of his companies in an attempt to avoid going bust. This joke was very topical at the time.

(274) The Green Green Grass continues the running joke from Fools and Horses that Tyler might be the result of a fling between Del Boy and Marlene.

(275) A 2020 documentary called Boycie in Belgrade saw John Challis travel to Serbia in an attempt to discover why Only Fools and Horses is so popular there. John drew large crowds at book signings in Belgrade and was treated like a huge celebrity.

(276) The grave of Del and Rodney's mother Joan is seen a smattering of episodes - though it doesn't always look the

same. In the last episode we see that Rodney has had the names of Joan's grandchildren Damien and Joan engraved on the tombstone.

(277) In the episode The Unlucky Winner Is, Del wins (until it all goes wrong) 1,000,000 Spanish Peseta and celebrates as if he's become a millionaire. 1,000,000 Spanish Peseta wasn't actually a lot of money though. It would have been a nice little sum but hardly something you could retire on.

(278) Richard Branson managed to get his mush in Miami Twice because the cast and crew were on a Virgin flight and he badgered them for a cameo.

(279) John Sullivan said he had fun writing Rock & Chips because it was set around the time that he himself was growing up.

(280) The interior scenes of The Green Green Grass were shot in front of a live studio audience at Teddington Studios.

(281) Rodney was kicked out of Art School because of a minor drug conviction.

(282) To this day the second part of Mimai Twice is sometimes listed as Oh to Be in England but that's an error. Oh to Be in England was the title of an episode of The Darling Buds of May and the Radio Times mixed them up and wrongly printed this as the title of the concluding Miami Twice episode.

(283) On the subject of the second episode of Miami Twice, while I'm sure this episode has its fans, many felt it was very silly and disappointing. It doesn't really feel like Fools and Horses with Del and Rodney in the United States (how

did Rodney get through passport control with his drug conviction?) and it plays like some ill-judged 1970s big screen spin-off. The plot also feels somewhat reminiscent of that terrible George & Mildred spin-off film where George Roper is mistaken for a ruthless criminal.

(284) Due to the popularity of Only Fools and Horses and his visits there, John Challis was made an honorary citizen of Serbia.

(285) Lammas Park Gardens in Ealing was used for the cemetery in The Yellow Peril. Apparently it proved too difficult to get permission to film in a real cemetery.

(286) On the set of the Trotter flat, they frequently changed the dinner table so that sometimes it was even garden furniture! The thinking behind this is that as Del Boy is a wheeler-dealer he is probably constantly selling the dinner table and pretending it is an antique!

(287) John Challis and Sue Holderness were both Londoners in real life. John was born in Bristol but his family moved to London when he was a baby.

(288) John Sullivan said the Trotters having a three wheeled vehicle is symbolic of the missing piece in their life - their mother Joan.

(289) The show is sometimes slightly consistent about what floor of Nelson Mandela House that Del and Rodney live on but it supposed to be the twelfth floor.

(290) The rioters in Fatal Extraction were students from a Bristol drama school.

(291) There are references to two horror films in Three Men, a Woman, and a Baby - The Creature from the Black Lagoon and Rosemary's Baby. Creature from the Black Lagoon (what a great name for a film) was released in 1954 and directed by Jack Arnold from a screenplay by Harry Essex. Rosemary's Baby is a classic psychological horror film written and directed by Roman Polanski, based on the bestselling 1967 novel of the same name by Ira Levin. This was a horror blockbuster and paved the way for films like The Exorcist and The Omen.

(292) John Challis made a guest appearance as Boycie on Državni posao in 2018. Državni posao is a Serbian comedy show.

(293) The hotel in Mother Nature's Son is the Grand Hotel in Brighton. This was where the IRA tried to murder Margaret Thatcher by setting off a bomb.

(294) In the episode Mother Nature's Son, Del is surprised to see that you can now buy bottled water in supermarkets. However, in earlier episodes of the show we've seen Del pouring mineral water into his drinks! This is what you could describe as a slightly continuity goof.

(295) John Challis said that Chain Gang was one of his favourite episodes.

(296) Corgi have done some little diecast models of the Reliant Regal van from the show.

(297) Time Out said of the Fools and Horses musical - 'By God, the show's storyline is stretched so thinly here, it practically squeaks. Sullivan and Whitehouse have tried to cram a crowd-pleasing 64 episodes of material into a plot

based on just one: 'Dates', in which Del meets his future wife, Raquel (played here with a lot of charm by Dianne Pilkington). The resulting experience is like a low-stakes drift through a Madame Tussauds exhibition and a greatest hits compilation. As Mrs Obooko, Melanie Marshall's soulful rendition of Simply Red's "Holding Back the Years", as Del is beaten up by the Driscoll brothers in a scene of sudden brutality, is powerful. This is one of too few moments where this production, entertaining as it is, finds its own feet and doesn't simply prop itself up against the past.'

(298) When Lennard Pearce died, John Sullivan said - "Writing a script without him was like trying to put my coat on with only one arm. It just didn't work anymore."

(299) The coach in The Jolly Boy's outing episode is a Ford R1014 Plaxton Panorama Elite MkII, PEL 915M.

(300) Caroline Ellis, who played one of the young women Del chats up in Go West Young Man, said that the cast and crew found it hard not to laugh shooting the scene and even though the show hadn't even come out or been finished you could already tell it was going to be funny.

(301) According to a YouGov poll, 89% of the British public have heard of David Jason. The most amazing thing about that poll is that apparently 11% of people have NEVER heard of David Jason. Maybe they don't own a telly?

(302) David Jason said the episode Heroes and Villains fufilled his childhood desire to play a superhero!

(303) David Jason filmed the 1996 Fools and Horses Christmas specials and new episodes of his ITV show A Touch of Frost at the same time. That must have been a bit

exhausting.

(304) David Jason was in his early sixties when he shot the last Fools and Horses specials.

(305) In the prequel show Rock & Chips, Grandad is homeless after getting divorced and moves in with son Reg. Grandad has to share a room with the young Del Boy. Del Boy and Grandad developed a bond of loyalty which we see in Only Fools and Horses.

(306) John Sullivan made a cameo as a drinker in The Nag's Head in the episode Time On Our Hands.

(307) David Jason said it was very emotional when they wrapped the last scene for Time On Our Hands because it was (or so they thought) the end of show. However, they did of course then come back five years later.

(308) The last three Fools and Horses specials started shooting in August 2000. The last one wasn't shown though until late 2003!

(309) Del, Rodney, and Albert were supposed to turn into cartoon characters in the closing shot of Time on Our Hands as they walk into the sunset. They didn't do this in the end though.

(310) The Green Green Grass mentions that Boycie's son Tyler is good mates with Damien Trotter.

(311) In 2023, Kevin Jones from Northumberland created an intricate model of the area where Fools and Horses takes place. There was even a little Nag's head pub!

(312) The boxer Ricky Hatton made a guest appearance in The Green Green Grass as himself.

(313) Nelson Mandela House is called Sir Walter Raleigh House in Rock & Chips.

(314) In the prequel show Rock & Chips we see that Joan Trotter is a big fan of the cinema and films. They provide an escape from reality and her troubles.

(315) The reason why Del Boy was able to move back into his flat in Nelson Mandela House in the last three specials is that he had never put the flat on the market because it wasn't a good time to sell a flat when it came to property prices. I like to think too the flat had such sentimental value and so many memories Del could never bring himself to sell it.

(316) The late Mel Smith played DI Thomas in two of the Rock & Chips specials. Sadly it was one of the last things he did.

(317) Grandad was a fan of The Dukes of Hazzard. This was an American comedy action show which ran from 1979 to 1985 about two 'good ole boys' who get up to various escapades designed to annoy the county commissioner Boss Hogg. The show sort of like a Burt Reynolds car chase comedy crossed with The Beverly Hillbilies.

(318) Paula Wilcox, who has done many things but is best known for Man About the House, played Marlene's sister Pertunia in The Green Green Grass AND Grandad's wife Violet in Rock & Chips.

(319) Gold is sometimes called the 'Only Fools and Horses'

channel due to the amount of times it has repeated the show.

(320) John Sullivan said it was really difficult writing Rock & Chips and working out how to make everything seem consistent with Only Fools and Horses when it comes to the Trotter's history.

(321) Four years before Fools and Horses began, Nicholas Lyndhurst interviewed David Jason on a kids TV show called Our Show. Little did they know that destiny would bring them together again in the future.

(322) When they were cast in Only Fools and Horses, David Jason had no memory of meeting Nicholas Lyndhurst on Our Show four years previously. Nicholas remembered it though.

(323) Grandad is supposed to be in his mid seventies in Fools and Horses but Lennard Pearce was about a decade younger than that when the show started. It is quite unusual for actors be younger than their characters - usually it is the other way around. Look at all those horror films where the teenagers are played by people who look like 30 year-olds.

(324) Trigger got his nickname because he is supposed to look like a horse.

(325) One of the reasons why Enn Reitel was in pole position for Del Boy early on is that he could pass for the brother of Nicholas Lyndhurst. In the end though the BBC agreed with John Sullivan that it didn't matter if Del and Rodney looked completely different.

(326) In Rock & Chips, Joan Trotter's place of birth is listed as Clapham.

(327) After the broadcast of Sleepless in Peckham in 2003, John Sullivan said the door wasn't completely closed on the show and it was possible there might be another special one day. He was clearly eager to avoid the 1996 mistake - where the episodes were clearly meant to be the last ever ones but turned out not to be. As it turned out though, Fools and Horses obviously did not return after 2003.

(328) You sometimes see Albert having a drop of rum in Fools and Horses but in reality Buster Merryfield was drinking Coca-Cola mixed with water.

(329) John Sullivan was never one of those people who complained comedy was much better in the good old days. He was always willing to praise new things he liked - like The Office and Peter Kay's Phoenix Nights.

(330) When Buster Merryfield sadly died, Nicholas Lyndhurst said - "He was a gentle, sweet-natured man and he will be greatly missed by everyone who knew him. He made the part of Uncle Albert a national institution."

(331) John Sullivan said, because of the high expectations, it was especially nerve-wracking when a Fools and Horses special went out at Christmas.

(332) The structure of Fools and Horses is that three generations are represented in the Trotter flat. You've got young Rodney, middle-aged Del, and pensioner Grandad/Albert.

(333) Buster Merrfyfield was a jungle warfare instructor

during the war.

(334) John Sullivan said that the Del/Rodney dynamic was sort of based on people he knew who had much younger brothers - who would, whether willingly or not, tag along with the older brother on ill-advised business ventures.

(335) The website Dan's Media Digest wrote of Rock & Chips - 'Overall, Rock & Chips wasn't a total disaster, but it felt like a pointless excuse for John Sullivan to revisit his biggest success, now that David Jason has called it quits and present-day adventures are impossible. It stands a chance as a regular series (hey, it's already better than Green Green Grass!), but I'd like to see it break from this special's faltering comedy-drama style and become a proper old-fashioned sitcom filmed in front of a live audience. I still say that's the best way to "scare" writers into ensuring there's something for people to laugh at in their scripts. Then let James Buckley move closer to the heart of the plot as Del Boy, and actually make an effort to give us a laugh per minute. As prequel ideas go, Rock & Chips was akin to George Lucas deciding his own Star Wars prequels should be trio of introspective, character-based dramas -- not really what we want, considering what worked before.'

(336) The Fools and Horses specials have been cleaned up and released on Blu-ray.

(337) The working title for Only Fools and Horses was 'Readies'.

(338) There is no 'canned' laughter in Fools and Horses - or any other BBC sitcom come to that. The laughter you hear is the reaction of a live studio audience.

(339) Missing out on Del Boy wasn't a tremendous hardship for Enn Reitel. His voice work on commercials and big American shows like American Dad has made him very wealthy.

(340) The fake gold worn by David Jason as Del Boy in the show had to be replaced a lot because it didn't last very long. The gold colours would quickly fade.

(341) John Sullivan said that Del Boy was inspired by dodgy wheeler dealers he knew who didn't have much money but always took pride in their appearance and clothes.

(342) In the Grandad funeral episode, Rodney chides Del for not mourning or appearing sad. Del opens up to Rodney and says he doesn't know how to mourn and so is playing up the Del Boy image as a sort of performance to protect himself from grief at Grandad's loss. It is moments like this which illustrate the depth of the show.

(343) Margate's relative closeness to London (about 65 miles) made it a traditional seaside jaunt for working-class Londoners. Cheap air travel changed a lot of that but Del Boy and his friends still enjoy Margate.

(344) Only Fools and Horses was one of the first shows to experiment with the format of the sitcom. It was elastic in its approach to running times and also bold in its blend of comedy and drama. This was evident when the show tackled the tragic and sensitive issue of miscarriage.

(345) There are a lot of Fools and Horses themed t-shirts and clothes online. Some of this stuff is not official or licenced - a fact which Del Boy would have sympathy with!

(346) One of Grandad's favourite shows is Crossroads. Crossroads was a soap opera set in a Midlands motel.

(347) Del Boy has taken a couple of beatings simply to protect Rodney. His loyalty to his brother and family means he will go to great lengths to protect Rodney.

(348) David Jason said he was often asked to record a message as Del Boy for someone who was poorly or even in a coma.

(349) When it comes to the Driscoll Brothers, Danny is slightly more reasonable while Tony is supposed to be a bit nuttier. You have more chance of striking a bargain with Danny than Tony. Danny will give you slightly more time to pay a debt.

(350) The two boarding houses you see in The Jolly Boys Outing have both been replaced by flats since that episode was made.

(351) David Jason said that when he made Fools and Horses he loved the show so much he couldn't wait to get up in the morning and start shooting.

(352) Nicholas Lyndhurst said that when he played Rodney he exaggerated his own lankiness and 'gawkiness' as part of the character.

(353) Del Boy's attempts to be fashionable contrast sharply with Rodney and Grandad - who often appear to wear the same thing all the time!

(354) It would probably to fair to say that for some people the last three specials struggled to capture the magic of past

glories and suggested the show should have been gracefully retired in 1996. Many people enjoyed them though.

(355) John Sullivan said that the BBC didn't like the first two series of Only Fools and Horses at all and were more than happy to axe the show. However, the second series was then repeated and got big ratings - which secured its future. This has happened with other comedy shows which went on to be famous. One Foot in the Grave and The Inbetweeners were both largely ignored at first but then picked up a cult following through repeats - thus securing their future.

(356) What saved Fools and Horses was that it was repeated on afternoons and many people encountered the show for the first time through these afternoon repeats. This was a happy accident caused by a strike at the BBC by technicians. Unable to show things like live horse racing or cricket, the BBC plucked Fools and Horses almost at random as something to stick on instead.

(357) When the repeats of the first two series started they frequently hit the top five most watched shows on the BBC. John Sullivan was amazed when he saw this. His show had gone from being a flop to a huge success - all thanks to a technician strike!

(358) On the 40th anniversary of Fools and Horses, UK Gold set up a pop up Nag's Head with 1981 beer prices. You could buy a pint of beer for 83p.

(359) Only Fools and Horses getting 24 million viewers in 1996 is all the more impressive when you consider that by then many people had satellite television and quite a lot of new channels.

(360) John Sullivan said that Fools and Horses morphing into Christmas specials (rather than have more series) was really a consequence of finding it so difficult to get a window where the cast were all available for an extended period. David Jason in particular was very busy with his ITV deal at the time.

(361) Time on Our Hands was the most watched television event in Britain until 2012 - when it was beaten by the closing ceremony of the London Olympics.

(362) In an interview with the Daily Express in 1997, Buster Merryfield said he was hopeful that Fools and Horses wasn't finished yet. "We said goodbye at the end of the filming but I can't think why. Everyone wants to do it again. Anything that draws 24 million people is not on the wane yet. The story is open-ended and I think there's more mileage in it."

(363) David Jason did a fair bit of lobbying in the late 1990s to get more Fools and Horses made. He was clearly not ready to say goodbye to Del Boy yet.

(364) Two of the last three specials were shot early in 2002. Only the first one was completed for Christmas 2001.

(365) Del Boy likes using the word 'cushty'. This is a slang word which means nice or excellent.

(366) Though he is a bit of a rogue when it comes to business, Del Boy is still a very lovable character and this is one of the keys to the success of Fools and Horses.

(367) David Jason visited the set of Rock & Chips to say hello and wish them luck.

(368) Scalextric have done little racing models of the Reliant van and Del's Capri.

(369) Terry McCann drove a Capri in Minder so you could say this is another link between Fools and Horses and that show.

(370) The BBC edited the Fools and Horses episodes for later repeats - which led to many fans complaining. John Sullivan's son Jim was among those complaining. He felt many of the edits were ridiculous and ruined a lot of the jokes. One example of the edits was the BBC removing Grandad talking about what a great actor 'Sydney Potter' (it was actually Harry Belafonte) is and how he always plays the 'black fella'.

(371) The famous chandelier scene was actually based on something that happened to the dad of John Sullivan.

(372) Time on Our Hands had half of all the available viewers in Britain watching it in 1996. In our fragmented modern entertainment age it is amazing to picture half the country sitting down to watch the same thing.

(373) Brazilian artist Gustavo Nénão painted a beautiful Only Fools and Horses mural on a wall in Peckham in 2019. However, two days later miserable gits (as Del might say) from the council had the wall painted black and the mural ruined. Locals were very annoyed about this because they thought the mural was fun.

(374) Gustavo Nénão said he had always been a big Fools and Horses fan. "I really like the idea of the series, ordinary people, real lives, financial problems and dreams. I think it's an excellent reflection of life."

(375) Del Boy's Capri 2 Ghia has a tiger-print interior.

(376) One of the reasons why Del and Rodney resonate as characters is that, like them, most of us have had times in our life where we feel like we are working hard but still getting nowhere.

(377) Kenneth MacDonald, who played Mike, sadly died of a heart-attack only weeks before he was due to shoot the new 2001/2002/2003 specials.

(378) Cassandra is younger than Rodney in the show but in real life Gwyneth Strong is older (two years) than Nicholas Lyndhurst.

(379) David Jason had met Lennard Pearce before Fools and Horses because they were both in two plays together some years before.

(380) David Jason said he especially loved doing the scenes in Fools and Horses where Del Boy is in the market trying to sell his goods.

(381) David Jason assumed the show would end when Lennard Pearce sadly passed away. John Sullivan managed to come up with a sensitive and poignant way though to acknowledge the loss of Grandad and keep the show going.

(382) The BBC were apparently not convinced that David Jason and Nicholas Lyndhurst were the right actors to front Fools and Horses but Ray Butt fought for this duo and was proved right when they turned out to have great comic chemistry together.

(383) One of the Reliant Regals used in Fools and Horses

later found a home in the National Motor Museum in Beaulieu.

(384) Although they played grandson and grandfather, David Jason was only 25 years younger than Lennard Pearce in real life.

(385) An early idea for Del Boy was that he would have big Elvis style sideburns. David Jason decided against this though.

(386) When the cast of Fools and Horses got bigger in the later specials they actually increased the size of the set of the Trotter flat so it was easier to shoot with more people in there. This is the sort of thing though that viewers wouldn't notice.

(387) Although he is obviously famed as a character actor, there is definitely a bit of Del Boy in David Jason's Pop Larkin in The Darling Buds of May. Pop is a bit cheeky and, like Del, a schemer and ducker and diver.

(388) The last three Fools and Horses specials were shot back to back to keep the production costs down.

(389) The little boy who gets David Beckham's autograph in the Beckham in Peckham Sports Relief special is Joe Sullivan - grandson of John Sullivan.

(390) The Trotter flat and The Nag's Head interior were the only two 'permanent' sets in the show maintained by the BBC. When the show finally ended and the sets were dismantled, David Jason said it was very poignant because the show now only existed on tape and in his memories.

(391) The character of 'Monkey Harris' is mentioned more than once by Del in the show but we never actually meet him.

(392) Only Fools and Horses is a bit inconsistent when it comes to Del Boy's age. He is generally supposed to be in his mid to late thirties when the show began.

(393) You can buy a 'Gold Millionaire' limited edition Corgi model of the Fools and Horses Reliant van. This will set you back over £100 on Amazon.

(394) You can buy Only Fools and Horses Top Trumps on Amazon.

(395) The Only Fools and Forces musical has a running time of two hours and 30 minutes. There is thankfully an interval should you need to use (as Del might say) the khazi!

(396) You can buy Only Fools and Horses beach towels and blankets.

(397) Sue Holderness said her favourite Only Fools and Horses episode was From Prussia with Love.

(398) John Challis did the same voice as Boycie as he did in his guest turn in Citizen Smith. John Sullivan told John he wanted Boycie to have the same voice as that previous (police officer) character.

(399) Peckham covers a large area of South London and takes in many diverse communities.

(400) The Green Green Grass seems to be going out of its

way to be completely different to Fools and Horses with its countryside setting and fresh slate of characters around Boycie and Marlene. It appears that John Sullivan didn't want to do a spin-off show which would draw direct comparisons to Fools and Horses.

(401) The Boycie spin-off show does not, perhaps to the disappointment of some fans, feature Boycie in London and show us what he gets up to as a car dealer. It is plausible to speculate that one of the reasons why they didn't go down this avenue is that a few years before Green Green Grass the Charlie Higson sitcom Swiss Toni revolved around a sleazy middle-aged car dealer and mined this territory. Another factor is that a big theme of Minder was the comical antics of Arthur Daley trying to flog dodgy cars on his car lot. Having a sitcom based around the comical escapades of a dodgy car dealer would not have been a very original idea in 2005.

(402) Buster Merryfield was much dapper in real life than Uncle Albert. In fact, Buster wore a crisp blazer to his audition!

(403) John Challis said The Sky's the Limit was one of his favourite Only Fools and Horses episodes.

(404) Despite playing the car dealer Boycie, John Challis said he knew nothing at all about cars in real life.

(405) Only Fools and Horses is the BBC's biggest selling show ever on VHS and DVD.

(406) The Danbury Mint released a Fools and Horses Del Boy Teddy Bear. Here's the blurb - 'Del Boy, one of the greatest comedy characters in British television history

appeared on our screens for the first time in September 1981. Soon, we'd all fallen for the charms of this ambitious, fast-talking market trader with his dodgy get-rich-quick schemes! Now, to celebrate 40 years of John Sullivan's "Only Fools and Horses" Steiff present Del Bear, their tribute to this icon of British comedy. Del Bear's glorious sandy-coloured fur is made from luxurious mohair. He has corresponding beige felt pawpads and an optimistic twinkle in his black button eyes. He looks proper "cushty" in his iconic faux sheepskin jacket, red polo-neck jumper and flat cap. He even wears Del's gold-plated initial 'D' pendant around his neck. Del Bear is being issued in a strict limited edition of just 3,000 pieces worldwide.'

(407) The December 29, 1996 Only Fools and Horses special is still the most watched episode of any show in British television history. Surprisingly, Fools and Horses has no other episodes in the top ten. Second place, which is again a surprise, went to a 1979 episode of the sitcom To the Manor Born - which attracted 23.9 million viewers.

(408) A Channel 4 poll, in which members of the public voted through the Channel 4 website, voted Only Fools And Horses as the most loved British sitcom.

(409) After the death of Lennard Pearce, John Sullivan proposed that an elderly female relative of Grandad comes to live with Del and Rodney as a replacement. David Jason was against this idea though because he felt the dynamic would be wrong. It is funny when Del insults Grandad and Albert but it might not have come across so well if Del was dispensing these sarcastic quips and insults at an old lady.

(410) Rodney's nightmare (where Damien has taken over the world) at the start of Heroes And Villains is largely

inspired by Cold Lazarus. Cold Lazarus was a 1996 dystopian television drama by Dennis Potter set in the future. It was the last thing Dennis Potter wrote and came out two years after his death.

(411) Sue Holderness and John Challis became good friends on Fools and Horses and would even go on holiday together with their families.

(412) You can now, should you desire, buy a Fools and Horses moneybox shaped like a Reliant van.

(413) Grandad said he has never had a garden but we know he does own an allotment.

(414) David Jason said that playing Del Boy and Jack Frost (in A Touch of Frost obviously) was like slipping on a comfortable pair of slippers. He really loved these two roles.

(415) Steven Woodcock, who played Jevon, said that he still gets recognised on the street thanks to Only Fools and Horses.

(416) John Challis said that although Boycie overshadowed the many other roles he played in his career he never felt typecast and considered it a blessing rather than a curse to be associated with Boycie.

(417) Rodney sometimes wears a UK Decay t-shirt in early episodes. UK Decay are a punk band who formed in 1978.

(418) Rolling Stone once did a ranking of the 100 greatest sitcoms of all time and although there were numerous British entries (like Blackadder, The Office, Derry Girls) in

the American dominated list there was no mention at all of Only Fools and Horses. This was clearly a consequence of the people who did the list being unfamiliar with Fools and Horses. The British sitcoms they tend to know in America are things like Fawlty Towers and Fleabag.

(419) The original title for Rock & Chips was Once Upon a Time in Peckham. Sex, Drugs & Rock 'n' Chips was also considered as the title. Rock & Chips refers to rock salmon - which was a cheaper alternative to cod at the chip shop.

(420) To this day, if someone is caught running some scam or selling dodgy or dangerous goods they are often called a 'real life Del Boy' in the newspaper report!

(421) When they shot the Batman & Robin outdoor scene in Heroes & Villains, the production strategically used their lights to make it impossible for any lurking photographer to get a shot of the actors.

(422) Of course these days, with high-tech mobile phones and the internet, it would be very difficult to keep something like the Batman & Robin scene secret. Pictures of Del and Rodney on the street as Batman and Robin probably would have gone online months before the episode came out.

(423) As we mentioned, though set in Majorca, there was no location shooting at all for The Unlucky Winner Is. The producers may have been inspired by Duty Free in this regard. Duty Free was an ITV sitcom which began in 1984 and ran for 22 episodes. It was very popular in its day. Anyway, Duty Free is set in Spain but was shot at a studio in Leeds! The last ever episode of Duty Free was the only time they ever actually shot anything in Spain.

(424) David Jason said that what appealed to him most about Fools and Horses is that it wasn't your bog standard sitcom. The characters had the depth of characters in a drama rather than mere sitcom characters.

(425) A few years before The Green Green Grass came out, there was a BBC3 sitcom spin-off from The Fast Show called Grass. In the show Grass the fast talking Londoner Billy Bleach (Simon Day) has to flee the capital for the countryside because he's grassed on a villain named Harry Taylor. Sound familiar? It is basically the same premise as The Green Green Grass! Andrew Collins, one of the writers on Grass, pointed out the obvious similarities when The Green Green Grass came out. Collins did suggest though that maybe John Sullivan had never seen Grass and had no idea his show was so similar to another BBC sitcom that had only JUST finished.

(426) David Jason said that, in preparation for playing Del Boy, he watched the traders at the market and observed their patter and selling style in action.

(427) John Sullivan, as with Fools and Horses, composed and sang the theme song for The Green Green Grass himself.

(428) The Green Green Grass was apparently cancelled in the end because the BBC felt it was too expensive to make with the outdoor shooting and the ratings it was getting didn't really justify sticking with it. It was pretty popular though at times and did better than many other sitcoms.

(429) The original conception for Del Boy was that he would have a big gold ring on each finger. David Jason vetoed this though because he felt that EVEN Del Boy

wouldn't be that tacky.

(430) A poll by Brightcove in 2018 named Only Fools and Horses as the old show that most British people like to watch repeats of. Other shows which polled highly were Friends and Mr Bean.

(431) The Green Green Grass was the first British comedy series to be filmed all in high definition

(432) Gaynor Ward, who played Janice in A Slow Bus to Chingford, was the real life girlfriend of Nicholas Lyndhurst when this episode was made.

(433) Harlech Tower in Acton (used as the exterior for Nelson Mandela House) is in a shabby state today and tenants have complained about the conditions. The tenants say that with rents as they are today in London they can't afford to move.

(434) The Trotter flat has three bedrooms.

(435) Movieweb ranked Only Fools and Horses as the 16th best British television show of all time.

(436) In the Rock & Chips episode The Frog and the Pussycat, Del Boy plans to make a film called Dracula on the Moon. You could say that Del is well ahead of his time because most horror franchises ended up doing a sequel set in space! Critters 4, Jason X, Hellraiser: Bloodline, Leprechaun 4: In Space.

(437) David Jason felt that Del Boy was a very short-sighted character because he puts all that time, effort, and energy into crackpot schemes that never seem to get him

anywhere. David felt that if Del directed this energy and focus into life in general and a 'normal' job he would be much more successful and better off.

(438) Del Boy endlessly tells Rodney variations on what their mother said on her death bed - many of them designed to cajole Rodney into doing whatever Del wants him to do in that specific episode. Sadly, we never got to see in Rock & Chips what Del and Rodney's mother DID actually say on her death bed.

(439) Roger Lloyd-Pack was once in Iceland (the country not the supermarket!) and, out of the blue, a stranger recognised him and shouted "Alright Dave!"

(440) David Jason said one of his favourite scenes in Fools and Horses is when Del movingly throws Grandad's hat down onto his grave and then we later learn the hat actually belonged to the vicar!

(441) The reason why the young Del Boy never got married and his early relationships didn't last is that he essentially came as a trio. Any woman who took on Del Boy would have to accept Rodney and Grandad too. Del Boy would never have left them to fend for themselves.

(442) In the Grandad funeral episode, Del Boy says - "Good old Del Boy, he got more bounce than Zebedee." Zebedee is a character in the kids TV show The Magic Roundabout. The Magic Roundabout first aired in 1964. It was created by Serge Danot and features a group of anthropomorphic animals who live in a magical world. The main character is Dougal, a shaggy dog, who embarks on various adventures with his friends. The other characters include Florence, a kind-hearted girl, Zebedee, a jack-in-the-box who has

magical powers, Brian, a snail, and Dylan, a hippie rabbit.

(443) John Challis played several different roles in Coronation Street in the 1960s and 1970s.

(444) In the Rock & Chips episode The Frog and the Pussycat, the young Del Boy uses his most famous catchphrase - 'Lovely, Jubbly'. Maybe this was the first time he used it?

(445) David Jason said the big difference between him and Del Boy is that Del Boy loves the hustle and bustle of the big city while he much prefers pottering about in his countryside garden.

(446) Del Boy is a big fan of a sheepskin coat. The late great football commentator John Motson used to wear one of these.

(447) Buster Merryfield appeared in a commercial for The Lost World: Jurassic Park dinosaur pop-up collectibles.

(448) In 2023, it was reported that an 'Essex trader' had got hold of the carpet used in the Trotter flat for the last three specials and had cut the carpet up into little squares which he was selling for £400 each as memorabilia. That's the sort of idea Del Boy would have come up with!

(449) In the episode The Russians Are Coming, Del and Rodney stumble across a do it yourself nuclear fallout shelter and decide to put it together. In reality a do it yourself nuclear fallout shelter would have offered no protection in the event of nuclear war - a fact which John Sullivan is well aware of. You could argue this episode is ahead of its time because it predates the television film

Threads and the Raymond Briggs graphic novel When the Wind Blows - which both (in terrifying fashion) highlighted the absurdity of homemade shelters and government advice in the event of nuclear armageddon.

(450) In the episode Mother Nature's Son, Del is selling Peckham Spring Water for 45p per litre.

(451) Kate Saunders (sadly no longer with us), who played Sandra in The Long Legs of the Law, said that as she was playing a police officer she based her performance on Jill Gascoine as DI Maggie Forbes in The Gentle Touch. The Gentle Touch is a police procedural drama series made by London Weekend Television for ITV which began in 1980 and ran until 1984.

(452) A business website once estimated that Del Boy's schemes lost the Trotters £17,000 in total in series three of Fools and Horses!

(453) The Green Green Grass is (almost) the name of a famous song. "Green, Green Grass of Home", written by Claude Putman Jr., and first recorded by singer Johnny Darrell in 1965, is a country song made popular by Porter Wagoner.

(454) John Sullivan named Del Boy going hang gliding in Tea For Three as one the scenes in the show he thought was the funniest.

(455) You can, naturally, buy Fools and Horses fridge magnets.

(456) When the Trotters became millionaires the precise sum of money they made was £6.2 million.

(457) In the early 1981 Fools and Horses episode A Slow Bus to Chingford, Del Boy acquires a bus and comes up with the idea of using it to give tours around London. A later episode of Minder in 1991 titled The Coach that came in from the Cold has a similar premise. In that episode Arthur Daley acquires an old police bus and uses it as a tour bus for tourists. Minder was a big influence on Fools and Horses but in this specific case it seems that Fools and Horses inspired Minder. Del Boy and Arthur Daley would probably say that great minds think alike!

(458) It is probably fair to say the character of Boycie is softened a bit in The Green Green Grass compared to Fools and Horses. Boycie is still sarcastic in the spin-off but he doesn't seem quite so abrasive.

(459) Del Boy has bamboo wallpaper in his flat!

(460) The late Fools and Horses producer Gareth Gwenlan said that although Harlech Tower in Acton was used as the exterior for Nelson Mandela House they rarely filmed in Acton because the area was considered too dangerous at the time.

(461) Del Boy doesn't have the best diet. He's fond of a breakfast fry-up.

(462) The first episode of The Green Green Grass drew 9 million viewers. By the time the show ended just over 4 million people were watching it. It seems that once the curiosity spike ended, some viewers were a bit disappointed to find it was nothing like Fools and Horses and - an appearance by Denzil aside - featured no guest stars from the base show.

(463) Gwyneth Strong was in 21 episodes of Fools and Horses as Cassandra.

(464) Del Boy's romantic interests often serve as catalysts for comedic and dramatic storylines in Fools and Horses.

(465) To this day, Only Fools and Horses remains popular through reruns and DVD sales.

(466) Although the reception to the last three specials was mixed and many liked the 1996 specials better as an ending, we did see Rodney become a father - which was a nice coda to the character.

(467) I don't know about anyone else, but I personally like to think that Only Fools and Horses and Minder take place in the same universe and that Del Boy and Arthur Daley have done a lot of business together. You can imagine Rodney and Terry McCann sitting on the sidelines sharing tales of the comic indignities that Del and Arthur have put them through!

(468) There is definitely something of Mr Micawber in the eternal optimism of Del Boy.

(469) Del Boy suffers from irritable bowel syndrome at one point in Fools and Horses - which is a relief to him because he feared something worse. Irritable bowel syndrome (IBS) is a common disorder that affects the large intestine (colon). It is characterised by symptoms such as abdominal pain, cramping, bloating, gas, and constipation.

(470) One difference between Del Boy and Arthur Daley is that Arthur is notoriously tight whereas Del Boy will spend money if he has it. Arthur has a slate at the Winchester Club

which he constantly avoids settling. Del Boy on the other hand is the sort of person who will happily buy you a drink in the pub.

(471) When they made the last ever Fools and Horses specials, Nicholas Lyndhurst was about the same age that David Jason had been when the show first began.

(472) The character of Del Boy is often described as a 'wide boy'. Wide boy is a British term for a man who lives by his wits, wheeling and dealing and dabbling in petty criminality. Another fictional example of a classic wide boy would be Private Walker from Dad's Army.

(473) There were a number of shows that appeared in the immediate wake of Fools and Horses and seemed to have taken some inspiration from it. Prospects was a comedy drama on Channel 4 in 1986 which starred Gary Olsen and Brian Bovall as two men on the breadline with entrepreneurial ambitions. They even drive a yellow van. Dream Stuffing was a Channel 4 sitcom from 1984 about two young women who live on the breadline in a London tower block - with a flat that looks a lot like the Trotter flat (only grottier). Dream Stuffing had a catchy theme song by the late Kirsty MacColl. The atrocious 1980s ITV comedy Up The Elephant And Round The Castle with Jim Davidson also seems to be trying to latch onto that working-class Fools and Horses popularity.

(474) Having a comedy set in a tower block was by no means a new idea. The second big screen spin-off from Till Death Us Do Part was titled The Alf Garnett Saga and had Alf and his family moving into a new tower block (which Alf hated because he was scared of heights). The big screen film of The Likely Lads had Terry Collier moving into a flat

high in a tower block. Tower block comedy tropes include the lifts never working and feral kids trashing your car while you are high above and helpless to intervene!

(475) Some real life 'wheeler-dealers' and car salesmen have complained that characters like Del Boy, Frank Butcher, and Arthur Daley give their industry a bad name!

(476) A website in 2021 calculated that it would cost Del Boy £585 to get his Reliant van insured today.

(477) Arthur Daley is similar to Del Boy in the way he gets phrases wrong ("The world is your lobster") and also proves to be out of his comfort zone whenever he attempts to hobnob with some toffs.

(478) The singer Katherine Jenkins once did a rendition of Hooky Street on the Jonathan Ross show.

(479) When the last scene was completed for Time On Our Hands, the cast got a standing ovation from the studio audience which went on a for a long time.

(480) One of the reasons why Fools and Horses morphed into specials is that John Sullivan felt the show would be fresher if he simply wrote a special when his muse was with him - as opposed to writing six or seven new episodes purely because he had a deadline.

(481) Steven Woodcock, who played Jevon, said that (no surprise here) The Jolly Boys Outing is his favourite episode. Everyone loves that episode.

(482) The BBC didn't want Big Brother to be the first episode of Fools and Horses because they didn't think it

was very strong. In the end though Ray Butt and John Sullivan managed to get around this objection and it did end up as the first ever episode.

(483) John Sullivan and David Jason said they were both puzzled by the muted reception to Fools and Horses at first because the nuts and bolts of what would become Britain's most popular show were in place straight away.

(484) David Jason went back to do more of Open All Hours not long into the run of Only Fools and Horses. David was in his forties at the time playing the delivery boy and general dogsbody Granville!

(485) John Sullivan got the idea for the episode A Losing Streak from the fact that his father used to have long gambling sessions.

(486) In the Beckham in Peckham skit, it is explained that David Beckham is helping out Del Boy because Del Boy laid on a bouncy castle for the birthday of one of David's children!

(487) David Jason and Nicholas Lyndhurst had a superstitious ritual of both having chips and beans in the BBC canteen before the recording of Fools and Horses in front of a live studio audience.

(488) Apparently, it is not uncommon for people to ask for the Fools and Horses theme to be played at their funerals.

(489) David Jason believed that a big factor in the success of Fools and Horses is that John Sullivan, Ray Butt, and himself were all from working-class London backgrounds and so had an instinctive feel for the world depicted in the show.

(490) A lot of the humour in Fools and Horses comes from Del's misplaced confidence in his own business acumen.

(491) Only Fools and Horses was a big hit in Serbia. Mucke, the Serbo-Croat name for Only Fools and Horses, means "shady business".

(492) David Jason said he was a bit frustrated by his career before Fools and Horses came along because he had reached the age of 40 without becoming a lead actor. He thought he was destined to forever be the comic sidekick.

(493) John Sullivan apparently got the idea for The Green Green Grass when he visited the countryside home of John Challis.

(494) A book called 'You Know it Makes Sense Lessons from the Derek Trotter School of Business (and Life)' was released in 2018. The book features Del Boy sharing tips on business and talking about his life. It was written by Jim Sullivan.

(495) Del Boy, Rodney, and Trigger are the only characters who appeared in both the first and last episode of Only Fools and Horses.

(496) You can now buy Only Fools and Horses cushion covers.

(497) David Jason's real name is David White. There was another actor named David White so David, inspired by the film Jason and the Argonauts, changed his named to David Jason.

(498) John Sullivan said it was actually important that

David Jason is much shorter than Nicholas Lyndhurst because if Del was a big burly chap the insults he often hurls at Rodney could have come off as intimidating or bullying.

(499) Del Boy called himself Derek Duvall when he joined a dating agency.

(500) The Danbury Mint released a Fools and Horses Uncle Albert Teddy Bear. Here's the blurb - 'John Sullivan's classic character Uncle Albert from the BBC comedy series "Only Fools and Horses" has been brought to life in teddy bear form by the talented craftsmen and women at Steiff. His glorious smoky grey coloured fur is made of real mohair – one of the most beautiful and sustainable natural fibres in the world. Available exclusively from Danbury Mint, Albert is being issued in a strict limited edition – only 3,000 bears can ever be made.'

(501) In the episode It Never Rains, Grandad mentions a man named Nobby Clarke. This is the name of the character that Kenneth MacDonald played in the seventies sitcom It Ain't Half Hot, Mum.

(502) The episode The Russians Are Coming was made when nuclear paranoia was still rife. At the time the Soviet-Afghan War was still going on.

(503) In the episode Hole in One, Albert tells Del and Rodney that Ted (Grandad) looked after him when he was a kid.

(504) John Sullivan left school with no qualifications and had a battery of jobs. His big break was getting a sketch he had written accepted for The Two Ronnies.

(505) Del Boy's lack of knowledge when it comes to history, languages, and literature is explained by the fact that he had to go out and earn money from a young age and so never spent much time in school.

(506) Raquel's real name is Rachel. This famously causes poor Uncle Albert great confusion.

(507) Del Boy will sometimes use the term 'brass' as an insult to men. Brass is Cockney rhyming slang for prostitute!

(508) If Del Boy doesn't know the name of someone he tends to call them 'John'.

(509) Del sometimes uses the word 'sod' as an insult. This word is less common these days.

(510) John Sullivan had to be creative with Del Boy's language and comedy insults because he obviously couldn't have the characters swearing like troopers. In reality, a character like Del Boy probably would swear a lot. The prison sitcom Porridge faced a similar challenge. In that show they used words like naff, naffing, and nurk to replace swearing.

(511) The most endearing thing about Del Boy is his optimism. No matter what happens he always thinks good times are just around the corner.

(512) There were two different Capri Ghia cars used by the production in the show as Del Boy's 'other' vehicle.

(513) One of the Capri Ghia cars used in Fools and Horses was sadly left to decay but the other was spotted at Elstree

Studios covered in dust and sold at auction for £28,000. A private collector later purchased it from the man who owned it.

(514) Though it didn't do great at first and flirted with being cancelled it is amazing how quickly Fools and Horses became a part of popular culture. By 1983 the characters were doing skits for Comic Relief and instantly recognisable and beloved.

(515) Ray Butt said he got the idea to cast David Jason as Del Boy after watching him in Open All Hours. I wonder if he watched the episode where Granville tries to be cool and wears a medallion?

(516) David Jason said the part of Del Boy was a dream for him because not only did he get to do comedy he also got to flex his dramatic acting chops.

(517) Nicholas Lyndhurst said in 2019 he never watches Only Fools and Horses because he doesn't like watching himself act and watching the show now would be sad for him because of the cast members that are no longer around.

(518) Perry Agajenoffa, president of the Only Fools and Horses Appreciation Society, appears an extra in The Nag's Head during Strangers on the Shore.

(519) Natal Road Allotments, Brighton was used as Grandad's allotment in Mother Nature's Son. By this stage in the show the producers were filming more and more stuff out of London because the show was so famous and popular they needed locations away from the capital where filming was less likely to be complicated by onlookers.

(520) Sarah Duncan, who played Lady Victoria in A Royal Flush, stopped acting in 1989 and is now a successful novelist.

(521) The Trotters belong to the working-class and are portrayed as trying to break free from their economic circumstances. The show often offers a satirical slant on the British class system, highlighting the struggles and aspirations of working-class individuals striving for upward social mobility.

(522) There were occasionally seven episodes of Fools and Horses in a 'season' rather than the traditional six (six episodes is usually the norm for a British sitcom).

(523) The Capri Ghia was made by the Ford motor company. The design of the Capri was based on the famous American car the Mustang.

(524) A connective link between David Jason and Nicholas Lyndhurst is that they'd both worked with Ronnie Barker before Fools and Horses. If he'd been a bit younger you could imagine Ronnie Barker playing Del Boy. He could have played him a bit like Fletch from Porridge.

(525) David Jason did commercials for the Abbey National building society in the 1980s. He played a character very much like Del Boy. The Abbey National is now called Santander.

(526) The real shooting location for the clothes shop that Del and Rodney visit in A Royal Flush is New Canal, Salisbury.

(527) Hanwell Community Centre was used as the dinner

and dance location in Cash and Curry.

(528) The title of the episode Strangers On The Shore is inspired by the 1962 Acker Bilk instrumental Stranger on the Shore.

(529) Rodney mentions Kevin & Perry in Strangers On The Shore. Kevin & Perry are teenage characters played by Harry Enfield and Kathy Burke in Harry Enfield's old comedy sketch show. There was also a Kevin & Perry big screen film.

(530) The registration of Del's Capri Ghia's registration number changes in the show - which is obviously a consequence of the fact that two different Capris were used by the production.

(531) Tobacco Road in Wapping, London is where Albert and Grandad grew up. It was once an area of working-class homes and dock workers. In the episode He Ain't Heavy, He's My Uncle, Albert goes back there and finds the area has been changed beyond recognition and now consists of yuppie apartment blocks.

(532) In 2010, a man named Nathan Williams was charged with fraud after he sued several London councils for negligence after falsely claiming he suffered falls. Williams was alleged to have got the idea from Uncle Albert in Fools and Horses

(533) Only Fools And Horses The Musical became the longest running production at the Theatre Royal Haymarket.

(534) Gwyneth Strong said that when she auditioned for

the role of Cassandra she had no expectation of getting the part.

(535) A common French phrase of Del Boy is "Bonnet de douche". This means shower cap!

(536) The Trotter flat was deliberately designed to be mismatched with chairs and sofas that come from different suites.

(537) The original plan for The Jolly Boy's Outing was that the characters were going to go to Southend. They obviously changed that to Margate in the end.

(538) In 2003, the phrase "Lovely jubbly" was incorporated into the new Oxford English Dictionary.

(539) John Sullivan said that Rodney being regarded as intelligent thanks to two GCEs was based on some chap he used to know who acted as if he was a highly qualified genius simply because he had two GCEs!

(540) Del Boy has been known to order a blackcurrant and pernod.

(541) Peckham is controlled by Southwark Council.

(542) In 2018, the IGN website ranked Only Fools and Horses as the 5th greatest British sitcom of all time. They had The Office in first place.

(543) The Looper website ranked Only Fools and Horses as the sixteenth greatest British television show of all time.

(544) The chandelier which was smashed in a Touch of

Glass was fake but still a very expensive prop. It actually cost £6,000 to make.

(545) Only Fools And Horses was rehearsed at a Hammersmith church hall and also the BBC television centre. If you watch behind scenes footage you can see David Jason running through a scene three or four times before shooting just to make sure it will be as good as possible.

(546) Denzil actor Paul Barber once visited a drama class to talk to the kids there. A very young Idris Elba was one of the kids. Idris later said that Paul inspired him to become an actor and they were all in awe of Paul because they'd seen him on the telly in Fools and Horses.

(547) One of Del Boy's most eccentric cocktails was Tia Maria and Lucozade!

(548) David Jason felt the first series of Fools and Horses was a bit 'scrappy' and that the show took a while to find its feet and get into top gear. This is certainly not uncommon when it comes to sitcoms.

(549) At the end of the 1996 episodes, Del Boy says 'this time next year we could be billionaires'. Many felt this would have made a perfect final line as a coda to the series - which it was of course originally meant to be.

(550) In Rodney's nightmare at the start of Heroes and Villains, set 30 years in the future, Keanu Reeves is the President of the United States!

(551) Sky once did a show about the best television finales. In the show they selected Time On Your Hands as one of the

best finales - completely ignoring the 2001-2003 specials!

(552) John Sullivan was apparently a bit unhappy with Christmas Crackers - the first festive special. John felt the episode came across as a rehash of Go West Young Man.

(553) The Danbury Mint released a Fools and Horses Rodney Teddy Bear. Here's the blurb - 'John Sullivan's classic character Rodney Trotter from the BBC comedy series "Only Fools and Horses" has been brought to life in teddy bear form by the talented craftsmen and women at Steiff. His glorious light-blond coloured fur is made of real mohair – one of the most beautiful and sustainable natural fibres in the world. His paw pads are made from beige-coloured felt and his tired looking eyes suggest he's worrying about the outcome of the next dodgy-deal that Del has got planned! Rodders looks totally "cosmic" in his trademark camouflage jacket, bright yellow t-shirt and red-checked lumberjack shirt. Every detail has been meticulously reproduced with the same love and care as the bear himself. Available exclusively from Danbury Mint, Rodney is being issued in a strict limited edition – only 3,000 bears can ever be made.'

(554) The early videos (VHS) of Fools and Horses which were released with the original Ronnie Hazelhurst theme tune are apparently quite rare and sought after these days.

(555) James Buckley did Rock & Chips and the third (and final) series of The Inbetweeners around the same time. There were then two Inbetweeners big screen films. It would probably to be fair to say that James, despite playing Del Boy, has never really escaped from the shadow of Jay Cartwright and The Inbetweeners.

(556) In Rock & Chips, Del Boy is 15 in 1960. In real life, David Jason was 20 in 1960 so he is a bit older than the character.

(557) You probably wouldn't say the Beckham in Peckham short film for Sports Relief is canonical. It would be a bit far-fetched to imagine that David Beckham is mates with Del and Rodney and helps them flog underpants at the market!

(558) The Green Green Grass has a double meaning as a title because the grass is indeed green in the countryside but Boycie is also a literal 'grass' as far as the Driscoll Brothers are concerned.

(559) John Challis said that in his younger years he was typecast playing coppers. John put this down to his hcight!

(560) Sue Holderness sounds nothing like Marlene in real life. Sue's natural speaking voice is quite posh.

(561) The songs in the Only Fools and Horses musical are as follows - "Prologue - O Furtuna", "His Name is Derek Trotter", "Only Fools and Horses/Hooky Street", "Now Now Grandad", "That's What I Like", "Where Have All The Cockneys Gone?", "The Girl", "Mange Tout", "Bit of a Sort", "Raining for Grandad", "Being a Villain", and "Lovely Day". Act II features the songs "Marriage & Love", "West End Wendy", "What have I let myself in for?", "Gaze Into My Ball", "The Tadpole Song", "Holding Back The Years", "Margate", and "This Time Next Year".

(562) You can buy an Only Fools and Horses Monopoly Board Game.

(563) The licence plate of Del's Reliant van is DHV 938D.

(564) Ben Smith played Damien Trotter in the last ever specials. He was later in shows like EastEnders and Skins. Ben is yet another Fools and Horses actor who was also in Doctor Who.

(565) Andrée Bernard played the Nag's Head barmaid Nervous Nerys in two episodes of the show. Andrée later had a regular part in the sitcom The Brittas Empire. She was also in Doctor Who.

(566) The Darling Buds of May was ITV's top show in its pomp - even beating Coronation Street in the ratings. At this time David Jason couldn't put a foot wrong. He was in the two biggest shows on telly.

(567) Lennard Pearce was in quite poor health when he made Only Fools and Horses. He suffered from hypertension and had trouble with his balance.

(568) David Jason was allowed to improvise some of Del Boy's dialogue when he is in the market trying to flog some dodgy goods out of a suitcase.

(569) Cassandra was born in 1966 but Gwyneth Strong was born in 1959 - making her seven years older than the character she was playing.

(570) John Sullivan apparently regretted writing the last three specials at times due to the poor critical reception they got in the media. By all accounts he came to appreciate the episodes in the end.

(571) Buster Merryfield's beard as Uncle Albert was real. In

fact, he credited that beard with helping him get the part!

(572) The TV channel Gold launched a petition in 2019 which asked for a gold statue of Del Boy to be erected on the site of Harlech Tower (which was used as Nelson Mandela House in the early series).

(573) You can buy bobblehead figures of the Fools and Horses characters on Amazon.

(574) You can find a fair bit of Fools and Horses fan art online. There's a great poster of Del and Rodney as Batman and Robin.

(575) John Sullivan's niece was a police officer. He said that some the plots in Fools and Horses were based on stories she'd told him about police cases!

(576) You can now buy Only Fools and Horses flasks and wallets.

(577) Some of the cast members of the show have made appearances at Fools and Horses conventions.

(578) A property website said that a Peckham flat like the one in Fools and Horses would cost two thousand pounds a month to rent today!

(579) The Rolls Royce Hearse in The Frog's Legacy was supplied by Altys Funerals in Blackburn.

(580) There is terrific 'straight' acting by David Jason in Strained Relations. His speech to Rodney about how he has played up the Del Boy image so long as a front he doesn't know how to do anything else and then the moment where

he sits down where Grandad used to sit and fights back tears for a moment.

(581) Del's Capri car is a rather bold shade of green.

(582) Fools and Horses is by no means the first sitcom to get a prequel. First of the Summer Wine ran for two series in the late 1980s and was a prequel to Last of the Summer Wine.

(583) Nicholas Lyndhurst complained in the media that the BBC cutting budgets meant that Rock & Chips was made quickly and for little money.

(584) The Grandad funeral episode was exceptionally poignant for David Jason and Nicholas Lyndhurst because they had only recently attended Lennard Pearce's real funeral.

(585) There was a six minute Fools and Horses sketch for Comic Relief in 1997. David Jason, Nicholas Lyndhurst and Tessa Peake-Jones appeared. This sketch marked the last appearance of Buster Merryfield as Uncle Albert.

(586) In hindsight, Sleepless in Peckham is clearly setting the stage for Rock & Chips. It's like a cloaked pilot for the prequel!

(587) Repeats of the 1996 trilogy got ten million viewers when shown by the BBC in 1998.

(588) David Jason had to axe one planned episode of A Touch of Frost from his schedule in order to find the time to make the 1996 Fools and Horses specials.

(589) Del Boy is clearly what you might plausibly describe as a Thatcherite. He believes in free enterprise and a small state not poking its nose into his affairs. The irony is though that Margaret Thatcher's Britain has done precious little for him and Rodney. Margaret Thatcher also said there was no such thing as 'society' - which is a sharp contrast to the bonds of community that Del Boy cherishes in Fools and Horses.

(590) John Sullivan said that after the second series of Fools and Horses went out he was on holiday in Hastings and got a call from his agent warning him that Only Fools and Horses was about to be axed by the BBC. Thankfully this didn't happen but it could have.

(591) When John Major was the prime minister his government once complained to the BBC about Del Boy reading the Daily Mirror in Only Fools and Horses. The government felt this broke impartiality rules to have Del Boy reading a Labour supporting newspaper! I bet they wouldn't have complained if this had happened on a show that didn't have 20 million viewers.

(592) Only Fools and Horses beautifully combined slapstick comedy, witty dialogue, and heartfelt moments to create a unique and entertaining viewing experience.

(593) Before the last three Fools and Horses specials were announced, it was an open secret that the cast wanted to do more. The BBC dragged their feet a bit by all accounts though.

(594) David Jason said that Del Boy is never aware that his clothes look a bit naff. Del thinks he's a very sharp and snazzy dresser.

(595) Nicholas Lyndhurst said he saw Rodney as quite an innocent and gullible sort of character because Del Boy has always protected him.

(596) Margate was one of the first seaside resorts, the first to have donkey rides, and the first to introduce deckchairs.

(597) David Jason said he has a couple of bottles of Peckham Spring water from the show as mementoes. David is said to have a net wealth of about £7 million so he won't have to sell them on eBay!

(598) Some fans of the show feel that the character of Cassandra often felt a bit inconsistent and vague.

(599) We clearly see that Boycie is terrified of the Driscoll Brothers when they go in the Nag's Head. Their reputation clearly precedes them.

(600) Grandad has both a colour and black and white television in Fools and Horses. In the early 1980s it was not unknown for people to still have a black and white television. Grandad has a third telly which needs to be repaired. Presumably his dream is to have three televisions playing simultaneously! This would have allowed him to have all the channels in one go. In 1981, when Fools and Horses started, Channel 4 had yet to be invented so there were only three channels!

(601) The phrase "Only fools and horses work for a living" apparently derives from old American comedians.

(602) Grandad is retired in Only Fools and Horses - though he does get roped into assisting in Del Boy's schemes. One of the last jobs Grandad had was as a security guard as a

warehouse. Predictably though he was fired after a janitor made off with numerous goods under his nose.

(603) John Sullivan was broke and had no work on the horizon when he got the go ahead to do Fools and Horses. This was a great relief to him because he'd just bought a house and had a young family to look after.

(604) You can buy a Del Boy themed soap on a rope online.

(605) Nicholas Lyndhurst was just 20 years old when he was cast as Rodney.

(606) David Jason has been dubbed a "national treasure" by the British media due to his long and successful career in entertainment.

(607) David Jason said it didn't really bother him that a number of actors were approached to play Del Boy before him. That's the way the acting business works. Many actors only got their most famous role part through someone else turning it down. Quite a few people turned down James Bond before they offered it to Sean Connery.

(608) In 2015, John Prescott said of David Cameron - "A Del Boy prime minister selling fake promises and knocked-off policies that fall apart like an old Robin three-wheeler on the motorway."

(609) Jim Broadbent said it was always a pleasure to go back to Fools and Horses and play Roy Slater again because there was a 'family' atmosphere on the set and the cast and crew were very nice.

(610) You can now, should you wish, buy a Fools and

Horses advent calender.

(611) Jim Broadbent once said in an interview that a 'Jack the Lad' character like Del Boy wasn't a good fit for him. "I didn't feel that It was quite right for me. I was probably too tall for a start and the Jack the Lad character was not quite my style. As it turned out David Jason was perfect and he played Del Boy far better than I could have done."

(612) You can buy a Fools and Horses jigsaw puzzle themed around The Jolly Boys outing.

(613) Voters on the Ranker website have Only Fools and Horses as the second greatest British sitcom. It was only beaten by Fawlty Towers.

(614) Jason Murugesu once wrote an interesting piece in The New Statesman about how Del Boy and Only Fools and Horses was popular with immigrant families because many in those communities could identify with Del. 'This was a man who desperately wanted to belong, failing to fit into the aspirational lifestyle of the 90s. Del Boy was like all the immigrants who laughed at his antics. They related to him even if he was a middle-aged white man."

(615) Only Fools and Horses, as a whole, has a rating of 9 on IMDB. This is the highest rating of any British sitcom. Fawlty Towers is the closest challenger with a rating of 8.8

(616) Rock & Chips shows us that Del Boy began his habit of mangling French phrases at a young age!

(617) Although Del Boy is a bit dodgy when it comes to business he does have a moral code. He would never, for example, get involved in selling drugs or guns. Del would

never rip off an old person either.

(618) You can buy Only Fools and Horses playing cards online.

(619) John Sullivan's writing has been praised for its clever wordplay and quick-fire jokes.

(620) The Trotter family's unbreakable bond is a central theme of Only Fools and Horses.

(621) Rodney's GCEs are in Art and Mathematics.

(622) Boycie lives on the (fictional) Kings Avenue - which is a place where rich people live. You wouldn't catch Boycie living in a tower block.

(623) The Reliant van is a central element of the show, often being involved in comedic mishaps and chases.

(624) Del Boy often has a note on the windscreen of the Reliant saying that the tax disc is in the post!

(625) In the episode The Frog's Legacy we see that Albert is aware that Freddie the Frog is Rodney's biological father but tries to keep a lid on this because he wants to protect Del and Rodney.

(626) Apparently, the Reliant Regal Supervan in real life was a very reliable vehicle and difficult to crash.

(627) Christopher Ryan, who played the diminutive gangster Tony Driscoll, has been in loads of stuff but is best known as Mike (the Cool Person) in the cult sitcom The Young Ones.

(628) Roy Slater's eternal bitterness from Del Boy stems from the fact that he was excluded from Del's gang of friends when they were teenagers because Roy was untrustworthy. He was also a police cadet and Del Boy and his friends definitely didn't want to knock around with the 'Old Bill'.

(629) It appears that Del Boy kept the Reliant van even when he became a millionaire and had a Rolls Royce. He just couldn't bring himself to part with it.

(630) Only Fools and Horses's success spawned several unofficial fan conventions and gatherings.

(631) Boycie's tipple of choice is a large cognac.

(632) Jim Sullivan wrote a 'biography' of Del Boy called He Who Dares. This book is worth a look for fans of the show.

(633) In 2022, it was estimated that there are about 250 Reliant Supervans still licenced and on the road in Britain.

(634) Del Boy was a Mod in his younger days. The Mods wore sharp suits, listened to British pop and American soul music, and rode scooters.

(635) The Fools and Horses title sequence represents the chaotic life of the Trotters and how money comes into one pocket and goes straight out the other.

(636) In their review of the first Rock & Chips special, The Independent wrote - 'Rock & Chips was a strange affair, a 90-minute amplification of one of the running gags in Only Fools and Horses, that concerning Rodney's dubious parentage. All the old gang - Del and Trigger and Boycie -

were on hand as schoolboys, but John Sullivan's drama was less interested in them than in the brief affair between Joanie, Del's mum, and Freddie "The Frog" Robdal, a career criminal, played here (naturally) by Nicholas Lyndhurst. Less interested, too, in straightforward sitcom than an unsatisfactory hybrid of classic Trotter cheekiness and something much more melancholy and heartfelt. The soundtrack was like an antique jukebox and there were some sly touches of period detail (a cigarette machine in a hospital waiting room), but the narrative's focus was blurred and the pacing weirdly off - quite a lot of the time you were well ahead of the drama and hanging around for it to catch up with you.'

(637) Apparently, about three actors read for the part of Grandad before they picked Lennard Pearce.

(638) There was no pilot episode of Only Fools and Horses. They just plunged straight into the series.

(639) David Jason said that while he is very happy and proud of the career he's had, his one regret is that he was never in a big Hollywood movie.

(640) The book He Who Dares suggests that Del picked up the Reliant van on the cheap after selling his old Mod scooter.

(641) John Sullivan used to work with a man who had the second name Trotter. This name obviously stuck in his memory.

(642) When Buster Merryfield sadly died, David Jason said - "He was a great man and a joy to work with and I will seriously miss him both as a friend and as an actor."

(643) When the new Fools and Horses specials were announced in 2001, the tabloids reported that each special had a production of budget of one million pounds.

(644) John Sullivan was a big Laurel & Hardy fan as a kid. He said this legendary comic duo were an influence on Del Boy and Rodney.

(645) In the episode May the Force Be with You, Roy Slater returns to Peckham. He is now a Detective Inspector and has been tasked with tracking down a stolen microwave oven. It is doubtful that a stolen microwave oven (which are as cheap as chips online) would plausibly occupy a Detective Inspector's time today!

(646) John Sullivan said the character of Harold Steptoe was a big influence on Fools and Horses. Harold dreams of a better life but is trapped by circumstances - both in terms of his family and his class.

(647) The character of Roy Slater is a retool of PC Tofkin - who was a bent copper from John Sullivan's previous sitcom Citizen Smith.

(648) David Jason recorded a little good luck message in character as Del Boy to the England football team during Euro 2020.

(649) John Sullivan's son Jim said that he would never allow Only Fools and Horses to be rebooted or remade as a television show but he is happy for the characters to appear in other mediums - like plays, stage shows, or books.

(650) The location for the farm scenes in The Green Green Grass was actually the real home of John Challis! John had a

rural house on the Herefordshire/Shropshire border.

(651) Del Boy made an animated cameo on The Apprentice in 2023.

(652) Jim Broadbent said, rather modestly, that his greatest contribution to British culture is turning down the part of Del Boy. Jim thinks he couldn't possibly have been as good as David Jason.

(653) One of the main reasons why the nation took Fools and Horses to its heart is that we all root for underdogs and Del and Rodney are classic underdog characters.

(654) A few BBC articles have suggested that Roger Lloyd-Pack was considered for the part of Del Boy before he was cast as Trigger.

(655) It was the BBC's Head of Comedy, John Howard Davies, who commissioned Only Fools and Horses. Davies wasn't too keen on the idea at first but came around in the end.

(656) What helped a lot with the genesis of Fools and Horses is that producer/director Ray Butt had, like John Sullivan, worked in street markets when he was younger. Ray had a good understanding of the world that John Sullivan wanted to depict in the show.

(657) George Wendt appeared in The Green Green Grass Christmas special The Special Relationship. Wendt famously played Norm in the classic sitcom Cheers. John Sullivan knew George Wendt because an American version of his sitcom Citizen Smith was produced next to the Cheers set.

(658) In Saturday the 14th, Del Boy jokes that the police helicopter is 'Barrets'. This is a reference to a television advert for Barret homes where the actor and voiceover king Patrick Allen sat in a helicopter flying over sites where Barret homes were due to be built.

(659) The viewing figures for Fools and Horses were so middling at first that it was often had less viewers than the BBC's niche sci-fi shows Doctor Who and Blake's 7.

(660) Grandad had a spell in the Foreign Legion. It didn't last very long.

(661) Del Boy is definitely a ladies man. We hear of many, many old flames of Del over the course of Fools and Horses.

(662) John Sullivan had intended to have a few comic scenes in Fools and Horses where Grandad takes his false teeth out (as Wilfred Brambell did in Steptoe & Son) but this was foiled by the fact that Lennard Pearce still had all his own teeth!

(663) Grandad's name (as we much later found out) is Ted but he was never called that in Fools and Horses. He was always Grandad or Mr Trotter.

(664) The Portuguese remake of Only Fools and Horses was called O Fura-Vidas. This remake stuck to the original scripts quite closely and is considered to be one of the better foreign remakes of the show.

(665) The interior decor of Del and Rodney's flat is certainly on the garish side with copious yellows and a shaggy carpet.

(666) Throughout the series, Del Boy and Rodney grow from naive dreamers into more mature individuals.

(667) David Jason and Nicholas Lyndhurst hit it off straight away on Fools and Horses and found it easy to work together. This was a great relief because the production wouldn't have been much fun if they'd disliked one another!

(668) Del Boy, Trotter, Denzel, Boycie and Trigger went to Dockside Secondary Modern school.

(669) The Nag's Head is quite a common name for a pub.

(670) In 2022, it was reported that a fan of the show in Essex had opened a mini restaurant called Only Fools and Sauces!

(671) The voice of Del Boy's late mother in Time on Our Hands was actually done by Tessa Peake-Jones.

(672) In the later episodes of Only Fools and Horses they had to dye David Jason's hair because it was grey in real life. This actually fitted the character though because Del Boy is certainly vain enough to dye his hair.

(673) Grandad and Uncle Albert fell out when they were young. They had a scuffle on the way home from a nightclub. The fight was over a girl named Ada - who Albert married in the end. After this Albert never spoke to Grandad again - although he came to regret this and wished he could have patched things up before Grandad died.

(674) David Jason was about 74 when he played Del Boy in Beckham in Peckham.

(675) John Sullivan originally intended to end Fools and Horses with a single solitary special in 1996 but the story got so large he found it impossible to tie everything up in one script.

(676) John Challis was a respected Shakespearean actor.

(677) The Times wrote of the Fools and Horses musical - 'Oh, there are moments of charm and skill in here. Del falls through the bar, as you want him to, but they teasingly make us wait for the moment. Whitehouse has fun sticking on a big white beard as Uncle Albert – more fun than he has as weary Grandad – and, yeah, so many of John Sullivan's original lines still sound lovely jubbly. They have a neat idea for Trigger (an amusingly lugubrious Peter Baker) to summon up the hipster Peckham of 30 years hence with a crystal ball. Then they fudge the execution. Del and Raquel's first date is funny, awkward and tender. And then, from nowhere, they start singing "Lovely Day" by Bill Withers. Eh? Can they do that? What are the rules here? It's a well-meaning evening but it needs a generous audience.'

(678) The first ever Fools and Horses Christmas special got lower viewing figures than the Doctor Who spin-off K-9 and Company. That was a bit humiliating I'd imagine! Fools and Horses had the last laugh in the end though.

(679) Nicholas Lyndhurst said that Grandad's speech about war in the episode The Russians Are Coming made him quite emotional.

(680) Rock & Chips started strong with 8.4 million viewers but the last special was watched by only 3.7 million. It could be the case that some people lost interest when they saw it was a period drama and not really a sitcom. For whatever

reason it didn't manage to hook viewers and maintain its audience.

(681) Some location shooting in Ealing was done for Go West Young Man. A few Peckham road signs were put up to maintain the illusion it was Peckham.

(682) John Sullivan said he invented the character of Cassandra because he wanted to give Rodney a happy ending.

(683) When he was working on the sitcom The Royal Bodyguard, David Jason met an amourer on the set who had served in Afghanistan. The former soldier told David when he was fighting in Afghanistan his platoon would watch The Jolly Boy's Outing episode when they got some time off because it was a way to escape from their troubles and situation for an hour.

(684) The inflatable dolls in Danger UXD are called Lusty Linda and Erotic Estelle.

(685) David Jason said that the character of Del Boy is much more confident than him.

(686) Del Boy will sometimes declare "Fromage frais!" when he's surprised or exasperated!

(687) The reason why they didn't do the Del Boy falling through the bar scene in The Nag's Head is that it wouldn't have made any sense for Del to fall through the bar there given how familiar he is with the place. It had to be a place he wasn't familiar with.

(688) John Sullivan said he didn't want cameos from Fools

and Horses characters in The Green Green Grass because then viewers might expect a full blown Fools and Horses reunion disguised as The Green Green Grass - a prospect which was never realistically going to happen.

(689) At one point, when 'Readies' was still the working title for what became Only Fools and Horses, they considered calling the show Big Brother. This idea was rejected though for its connections to George Orwell's 1984.

(690) John Sullivan said that the 2001-2003 specials happened because the producer Gareth Gwenlan gave an interview saying the show was coming back and so they were 'forced' into it because they didn't want to let anyone down.

(691) The exterior of the Theatre Royal, Drury Lane was used in A Royal Flush. For the interior theatre scenes they used the Buxton Opera House.

(692) Del Boy likes Brut aftershave/cologne. The boxer Henry Cooper used to advertise this on the telly.

(693) The Stage, in their review of the Fools and Horses musical, wrote - 'Carol Jay Ranger's production is both an exercise in nostalgia and a lament for a London lost, recreating a world populated by barrow boys and small-time villains – the denizens of the Nag's Head. It doesn't really work as a musical though. The songs include a couple of Chas and Dave numbers, as well as Sullivan's own ear-worm theme song and some much less catchy numbers supplied by Whitehouse, but it all feels a bit cobbled together. The charm of the cast go a good way to salvaging things. Bennett miraculously manages to make David Jason's verbal tics and malapropisms – all the "bon jours"

and "mange touts" – his own, while layering on the charm and warmth.'

(694) An American reviewer, unfamiliar with the show and writing about the first three seasons of Fools and Horses for DVD Talk, wrote -

"With all the love, all the accolades, this intrepid reviewer (who had never seen the show before) was skeptical. Really skeptical. This kind of extreme love for an unseen program always seems to result in apathetic disappointment. Thankfully, I needn't have worried. Only Fools and Horses not only came across as a warm and deeply funny program, it's simply a great show. Only Fools and Horses is set in working-class Peckham, and the show was centered on the comedic misadventures of the Trotter brothers, Del (David Jason) and Rodney (Nicholas Lyndhurst). Living in a cramped, dingy flat with their Grandad (Lennard Pearce), the duo eked a living mostly through cons and scams, using whatever resources they can in order to make a fast buck. Del, the older brother, is the smarter and more conniving one, always the wheeler-dealer, while simple, big-hearted Rodney is the slightly more sensitive soul of the pair.

Great television comedies come about through clever scripts and memorable characters, and Only Fools and Horses provides those in abundance. The barbed but good natured rapport between Del and Rodney is pretty much irresistible. The principal performers, who resemble Nathan Lane and the kid who played Nelson in Spring Break (respectively), are so believable and endearing in their roles that, after watching the first two episodes, I was instantly hooked. This is truly a wonderful show.'

(695) Del will sometimes call someone a 'saucy git'! This is

used in response to someone being cheeky or sarcastic to him.

(696) YouGov polling in Britain ranks Only Fools and Horses as the most popular show of all time. Fawlty Towers was second.

(697) Nicholas Lyndhurst said that when he got the first ever Fools and Horses script he sat up until two in the morning reading it in bed.

(698) Les Dennis has played Grandad in the Fools and Horses musical. On the appeal of the television show, Les Dennis said - "It captures that dysfunctional family we can all relate to and their aspirations. It's got great comedy but it's got great heart. People identify with the characters. We all think we know a Del Boy or we've got a Grandad in our family."

(699) The Reliant van belonging to Del definitely has a dodgy exhaust. Look at that smoke!

(700) The American actor Steve Carell (star of many films and the US version of The Office) told Empire Magazine in 2010 that his dream role was to play Del Boy in an American version of Fools and Horses. I suspect he was probably joking.

(701) One of the great things about Fools and Horses is that as it went on it juggled an increasingly large cast but made all the characters vivid and funny. This is difficult to do but John Sullivan made it look easy.

(702) Only Fools and Horses went out on a Tuesday when it first aired (Tuesday was not a great timeslot - which may

partly explain the mediocre early ratings). It was then moved to Wednesday. When it became really huge it was moved to Sunday.

(703) Del Boy will sometimes call someone a 'wally'. This is slang for a stupid person. The origins of this term allegedly come from a music festival in 1970 where the crowd were amused by the loudspeaker endlessly requesting that someone called Wally come to the office. The crowd must have presumed that Wally was some daft person who got lost - so started using 'wally' as an insult thereafter.

(704) Empire Magazine ranked Only Fools and Horses number 42 on their list of the greatest television shows of all time.

(705) Duke is the name of Marlene and Boycie's Great Dane dog.

(706) John Sullivan said he based the Trotters on his own family and friends. He had first hand experience of people not having much but trying their hardest to improve their circumstances against the odds.

(707) Grandad did some gun-running in Spain during the Civil War!

(708) John Sullivan said that reading David Copperfield as a kid was the thing that gave him a passion for writing and stories. The story in the novel charts the life of the title hero from birth to maturity and what a tale it turns out to be. David suffers loss, is orphaned, adopted, experiences child labour, falls in love, is betrayed, and, well, you'll just have to read it for yourself to see if everything turns out ok for David Copperfield in the end. There can surely be few books

in the history of literature with so many vivid and memorable supporting characters as David Copperfield has. The oleaginous Uriah Heep, the incomparable Wilkins Micawber (who, despite his financial woes, is always sure that something wil turn up), the ever loyal Clara Peggotty, the awful Murdstones (surely among the most despicable human villains to grace any novel), the unforgettable Betsey Trotwood, the charismatic but distrustworthy James Steerforth, and the humble but heroic Daniel Peggotty. And this is only the tip of the iceberg! There are far too many great characters to mention. If you've never got around to reading any books by Charles Dickens then there is probably no better place to start than David Copperfield.

(709) Del sometimes uses the term 'monkey' in relation to cash. Monkey means £500.

(710) It was often quite difficult to get new episodes/specials of Fools and Horses made in the early 1990s because David Jason and John Sullivan were both so busy with other things.

(711) Del Boy will sometimes say he's been 'done up like a kipper' - which means tricked or caught red-handed. The origins of this phrase have never quite been established. Something to do with fish being smoked presumably.

(712) John Sullivan said they never once considered recasting the part of Grandad when Lennard Pearce died. They felt that would have been disrespectful. They - sensibly - decided instead to bring in a completely new character who was related to Grandad.

(713) Del Boy will sometimes exclaim "Gordon Bennett!" This is an old phrase used to express surprise.

(714) Del Boy once ordered a brandy and cream soda!

(715) One of Rodney's favourite words to use is 'cosmic'. This is often deployed with sarcasm.

(716) When they shot Only Fools and Horses scenes outdoor in Bristol they would try to bung a red bus in the background to make it look like London.

(717) Del Boy purchased his Capri from Boycie for £400.

(718) They added stains and bits of food to Lennard Pearce's clothes as Grandad to make him look as dirty and unkempt as possible!

(719) The BBC's Points of View (a show where letters from viewers are read out) got complaints about the episode A Royal Flush when it went out. A lot of viewers complained that Del Boy came off as too nasty in this episode.

(720) Grandad wears his pyjamas under his clothes. This tends to suggest that he rarely washes his clothes or gets dressed!

(721) Rodney and will often say 'terrific' - which he will pronounce as 'triffic'. As ever with Rodney, the word will often be deployed in a sarcastic fashion.

(722) The late great footballing legend Jimmy Greaves was a big Fools and Horses fan. He would give the show a glowing review when he used to do TV reviews on breakfast telly.

(723) Del Boy often calls Rodney by the nickname 'Rodders'.

(724) Filming on the first ever episode of Fools and Horses began in May 1981.

(725) You can book an Only Fools and Horses Tour in Bristol which takes you around the city by coach and stops at locations used in the show. At the time of writing it costs £32 (for adults) to go on this tour. The reviews seem to be pretty good.

(726) David Jason said that if they did a night shoot on Fools and Horses the director/producer Ray Butt would put little bottles of gin and tonic in his coat to drink!

(727) You can find traditional pie and mash eateries in Peckham. The jellied eels are a bit more of an acquired taste!

(728) Gerry Cowper appeared in two episodes (Tea For Three and The Frog's Legacy) as Boycie's niece Lisa. Horror fans might be interested to know that as a child actor Gerry played Rowan - the 'missing' girl who drives the plot of the cult classic 1973 folk horror film The Wicker Man.

(729) Del Boy will often say 'mange tout' - not knowing that it means pod peas!

(730) Del Boy would often try to entice Mike the landlord into buying his goods. This mirrored Minder - where Arthur Daley would try to tempt Dave (the owner and barman at the Winchester Club) into buying things. Dave usually had the good sense to say no!

(731) The character of Rose Tyler in Doctor Who lives in a Peckham tower block. This might well have been influenced by Fools and Horses. Maybe Rose Tyler met Del and Rodney

a few times!

(732) Denzil's full name is Denzil Tulser.

(733) In 2023, the We Got This Covered website ranked Only Fools and Horses as the second great British comedy show of all time. They had Brass Eye in first place.

(734) Boycie is (or at least was) a Freemason. "What d'you wanna join that bunch of dipsticks for?" is Del's response to hearing that news!

(735) The Trotter flat is very dark in series one. From series two onwards they brightened the flat set up a bit.

(736) Marlene used to work in a betting shop.

(737) Although we know of some actors who were considered for Del Boy before David Jason, it seems that no one else was in serious contention to play Rodney and Nicholas Lyndhurst was settled on very early in the casting.

(738) We see in the Margate episode that Del is partial to a bit of scampi.

(739) When the first series of Fools and Horses went out, the king of the BBC sitcoms was To the Manor Born - which drew audiences of over 15 million. Only Fools and Horses would eventually become even more popular than To the Manor Born.

(740) One of the reasons why Raquel and Cassandra were introduced is that John Sullivan wanted more female characters in regular roles.

(741) John Sullivan wrote the episodes in the first series before he knew who was going to play Del and Rodney. He said he did some reworking of the scripts when David Jason and Nicholas Lyndhurst were cast in order to tailor them for these specific actors.

(742) Grandad rarely seems to leave the Trotter flat. In fact, he rarely leaves his armchair!

(743) One advantage that Minder (in the Dennis Waterman years) had Over Fools and Horses is that Minder did extensive location shooting in all parts of London and so had more of an authentic London atmosphere than Fools.

(744) John Sullivan said the seed for Fools and Horses came from his youth when he would notice unlicenced traders flogging dodgy goods out of a suitcase in the market. These fly by night traders had to have the gift of the gab and they also had to have the ability to leg it at a moment's notice!

(745) When the first series of Fools and Horses went out, John Sullivan was very frustrated by what he saw as a lack of promotion by the BBC - who seemed to have little interest in the show initially.

(746) Del Boy's favourite band is The Who.

(747) Nelson Mandela House has twenty-six levels.

(748) Del Boy often says "You know it makes sense" when he is trying to cajole Rodney into agreeing to something.

(749) David Jason is a Londoner in real ife. Nicholas Lyndhurst on the other hand was born in Hampshire.

(750) Another of Del's catchphrases is "Shut up you tart!" David Beckham said this line in the Beckham in Peckham special.

(751) In the episode where Rodney gets married and Del is alone at the end with the song Holding Back the Years playing, David Jason said that he got a bit choked up for real.

(752) David Jason said he hates soap operas because the characters in them are usually having a terrible time and there is rarely much humour.

(753) Rodney's middle name is Charlton. His mother obviously supported Charlton Athletic and liked Charlton Heston.

(754) David Jason only took the plunge and gave up his day job to become an actor when he was 25.

(755) A five-minute spoof BBC documentary was broadcast on Breakfast Time on 24 December 1985. In the documentary Del being investigated by a BBC consumer expert.

(756) David Jason's versatility as an actor is evident by the fact that he played Del Boy and the long suffering delivery 'boy' Granville in Open All Hours around the same time. You could not think of two characters that were more different. In this, David took after his mentor Ronnie Barker (it's hard to believe the same person played Arkwright in Open All Hours and Fletch in Porridge!)

(757) There were a lot of myths about Reliant three-wheelers. It was said that they couldn't go round corners or

go on motorways but none of this was true.

(758) David Jason said he was very shy as a teenager and used acting as a way to combat this. He found his shyness went away when he was hiding behind a character.

(759) The Reliant van belonging to Del had rust but in reality these fibreglass vehicles were incapable of producing rust.

(760) David Jason said that he could never quite get his head around how popular and beloved Fools and Horses and Del Boy are by the public.

(761) Lennard Pearce was in the 1980 Hammer House of Horror episode Witching Time. The first time I watched that episode it was a bit of a shock to see Grandad from Only Fools and Horses turn up playing a vicar!

(762) A 2001 poll by Channel 4 ranked Del Boy as the 4th greatest television character of all time.

(763) In 2012, a blue plaque was unveiled by David Jason at Teddington Studios to celebrate John Sullivan's mighty contribution to British comedy.

(764) The spin-off show planned with Nicholas Lyndhurst when David Jason suggested he wanted to leave after series five, was going to have Rodney and Mickey Pearce taking over Trotter's Independent Traders.

(765) Nicholas Lyndhurst, who admits to being a very private and shy person, often wears a baseball cap in public to lessen the chances of being recognised.

(766) You see a Crystal Palace scarf in Del Boy's flat in one episode but they never mention him being a Palace fan in the show.

(767) David Jason said he loved shooting the second part of Miami Twice because they got to stay in a plush hotel. A cushty hotel as Del would say!

(768) Lennard Pearce did a play in Germany in the 1930s and afterwards some Nazi officials went backstage to congratulate the actors on their performance. One of the officials who congratulated Lennard was Adolf Hitler. Lennard told Nicholas Lyndhurst that if he'd known then what Hitler would go to do he'd have tried to kill him.

(769) A poll by Travelodge in 2023 found that 73% of the British public still watch Only Fools and Horses quite frequently. In case you were wondering why Travelodge were doing Fools and Horses polls, they had just opened one of their lodges in Peckham smack bang in the area where Del Boy and Rodney lived.

(770) The infamous "Chandelier scene," where Del Boy accidentally triggers a falling chandelier, was voted the greatest British TV comedy moment in a 2004 poll.

(771) The Travelodge poll voted Del Boy the best character. Trigger was second and Rodney was third.

(772) One difference between Del Boy and Arthur Daley is that Arthur keeps all of his merchandise and unsold goods at his lock-up warehouse whereas Del seems to keep his stuff at his flat!

(773) Del Boy's catchphrase 'Lovely Jubbly' derives from

Jubbly ice-lollies/fruit juice - which were marketed with that phrase when Del was young.

(774) Miami Twice is obviously a pun based on the famous American television show Miami Vice.

(775) Gold tend to make edits to Fools and Horses when they show it now. Swear words, for example, are edited out.

(776) Gwyneth Strong said that when she first got the part of Cassandra she was initially only booked for one episode and had no idea she was going to become a regular in the show.

(777) The second Miami Twice episode was shown with no laughter track. One was added for the DVD release. Opinions seem mixed on which version is better. It feels weird without the laughter track but by the same token the added on laughter track feels a bit fake and drowns out some of the jokes.

(778) The title of the episode Three Men, a Woman and a Baby is a pun on the film Three Men and a Baby - which was a big box-office hit in 1987.

(779) In 2023, the snooker star Ronnie O'Sullivan told the media that rather than practice he relaxes before a match by watching Only Fools and Horses on his phone!

(780) The 1983 episode Thicker than Water was also the name of a 1935 Laurel & Hardy short film.

(781) A former cameraman on Fools and Horses took home three bottles of the Peckham Spring Water 'props' but threw them away. That was a huge mistake because they

can go for thousands of pounds at auctions today.

(782) There are two Fools and Horses episodes with James Bond themed pun titles - From Prussia with Love and Diamonds Are for Heather.

(783) One of the Miami Twice episodes was broadcast at the same time as The Darling Buds of May on ITV. There was no escape from David Jason!

(784) The episode title Fatal Extraction is obviously a pun on the 1987 thriller film Fatal Attraction.

(785) David Jason was very apprehensive about doing an episode (Strained Relations) which dealt with the funeral of Grandad as he wasn't sure this sort of thing would work in a sitcom. David's wariness about doing a funeral episode eased when he read the script and saw how movingly John Sullivan had handled what was a delicate and difficult task. The episode was not only a fitting tribute to Lennard Pearce and Grandad and very moving but it also managed to be funny too. Roy Clarke pulled off something similar much later in Last of the Summer Wine when he wrote the episodes which dealt with Compo's death after Bill Owen passed away.

(786) In the episode Rodney Come Home, where Del Boy tells Albert to look horrified at the thought of Rodney going out with another woman, you can see that David Jason is cracking up for real.

(787) Phoebe de Gaye was the costume designer on Fools and Horses who designed the fashions that Del Boy, Rodney, and Grandad would wear.

(788) David Jason said that being considered a good actor was always more important to him than fame or money.

(789) Peter Woodthorpe, who played Del Boy's father Reg in Thicker than Water, was only nine years older than David Jason in real life.

(790) David Jason said that someone at the BBC wanted to show Del and Rodney as Batman & Robin in the trailer for Heroes and Villains and this had to be fought against because it was a stupid idea which would have ruined that scene by spoiling the surprise!

(791) A poll on the website Episode Ninja ranked Tea for Three as the funniest Fools and Horses episode.

(792) David Jason said he wasn't too fond of the Reliant Regal in the show because it was quite smelly and dirty to sit in and a pain to drive.

(793) The former chief inspector of schools Chris Woodhead called Del Boy a bad role model for children during the vintage Fools and Horses era. John Sullivan was annoyed by this and responded in the media. As he pointed out, Del Boy has raised his brother and looked after his elderly grandfather. That would surely make him a good role model for children wouldn't it? It isn't as if Del Boy is a dangerous criminal. He's just a ducker and diver trying to get by.

(794) Buster Merryfield said his forgot his lines the first time he had to record scenes for Only Fools and Horses. He said he felt better when David Jason then forgot some of his lines. Buster believed that David did this on purpose to make him feel better - which was a nice thing to do.

(795) Another of Del Boy's favourite insults is to call someone (usually Rodney) a 'twonk'.

(796) Roger Lloyd-Pack was in 39 episodes of Fools and Horses as Trigger.

(797) The cocktails that Del Boy drinks in the show were in reality made from mixing different fruit juices together. This was so that David Jason could actually drink a bit of them for a scene.

(798) David Jason said he always turns down scripts that have swearing. He said he doesn't like bad language on television.

(799) Rodney's Art School was in Basingstoke.

(800) David Jason wanted to do the hang gliding himself in the episode Tea for Three as hang gliding was one of his hobbies but the insurance people wouldn't allow him to do it.

(801) The BBC hated the title Only Fools and Horses but they couldn't think of anything better so it stuck - much to the relief of John Sullivan.

(802) David Jason said that he and John Sullivan asked the BBC for the episodes to be longer because they got fed up having to cut dialogue in order to keep to the 30 minute sitcom format.

(803) John Sullivan said he was so nervous when he had to sing the theme song in the recording studio he drank nine pints of beer.

(804) Trigger was supposed to be in the Beckham in Peckham Sports Relief special but sadly Roger Lloyd-Pack's health prevented him from doing it.

(805) In the episode A Losing Streak, Grandad doesn't seem to know who Boycie is. This contradicts the fact that Boycie is supposed to be one of Del's childhood friends.

(806) Lennard Pearce was thinking about retiring from acting before the part of Grandad in Only Fools and Horses came his way.

(807) John Sullivan said he brought the character Raquel Turner back and made her a regular because he thought Del was getting a bit old to be gallivanting around as a single-man man chatting up women in discos.

(808) Sue Holderness (Marlene) appeared in a 1984 Minder episode A Number of Old Wives Tales. Gwyneth Strong was also in Minder. She was in the episode titled Juror in 1982.

(809) The shooting location for Ridgemere Hall in A Touch of Glass was Clayesmore School in Iwerne Minster, Dorset.

(810) It was the producer Ray Butt who had the idea of casting David Jason as Del Boy. David would mimic Ray's London accent - which led Ray to suspect he might be capable of playing Del Boy.

(811) Del has been known to order a Baileys and cherryade. Sounds revolting!

(812) Nicholas Lyndhurst said he loved getting a new Fools and Horses script by John Sullivan and would always start reading it straight away.

(813) In the episode It Never Rains, Grandad mentions that the Trotters have never been good sailors. This (unwittingly) anticipates the arrival of Uncle Albert into the show later.

(814) Nicholas Lyndhurst said he doesn't mind at all that Only Fools and Horses will always overshadow the other stuff he does in his career. Nicholas said he is very proud to have been in one of the most beloved shows in British television history.

(815) In the episode A Losing streak, Del Boy mentions Buzby. Buzby was a cartoon bird who featured in British Telecom adverts of the era.

(816) David Jason said in 2023 that while he would love to play Del Boy again it would be impossible without John Sullivan and the cast members who are no longer around.

(817) Nicholas Lyndhurst actually starred in a fair few other sitcoms during the Fools and Horses era. The Two of Us and The Piglet Files on ITV have been largely forgotten but Nicholas did enjoy more success with Goodnight Sweetheart on the BBC.

(818) There is an urban myth that Robbie Williams was was an extra in the 1992 Christmas episode Mother Nature's Son. He wasn't.

(819) Del drinking daft cocktails give an insight into his character. He wants to come across as sophisticated but doesn't have the ability to do this convincingly.

(820) The production of the second Miami Twice episode (which was filmed in America) was nearly shut down by the

Teamsters Union because they were annoyed the BBC were not using their members as crew. The International Brotherhood of Teamsters (IBT) is a labour union in the United States and Canada.

(821) Rodney's nightmare sequence, where the adult Damien has turned Mandela House into Trotter Towers and is wealthy and powerful, owes something to Back to the Future Part II - where Marty McFly visits an alternate 2015 and finds that the villain Biff Tannen has become rich and powerful and lives in a big penthouse.

(822) David Jason and Arthur Daley actor George Cole actually appeared together in a 2007 crime show called Diamond Geezer. Diamond Geezer didn't do very well though and has been largely forgotten these days.

(823) Del Boy compares Rodney and Albert to Zippy and Bungle in The Jolly Boy's outing! These are characters from the kids TV show Rainbow.

(824) John Sullivan said he was rather dismayed when he saw the ITV show Minder because he thought it might have gazumped his idea (which would obviously become Only Fools and Horses) for a comic show about working-class London wheeler dealers.

(825) Del Boy largely operates in what is known as the black economy. Cash in hand deals which are hidden from the taxman.

(826) A poll for The One Show to mark the 100th birthday of the BBC voted Only Fools and Horses as the nation's favourite ever BBC show. Doctor Who was in second place.

(827) The character of Sid made his first appearance in The Long Legs of the Law.

(828) A Fools and Horses fan named Saso Zibert was featured in the newspapers in 2022 because he had lovingly recreated famous scenes from the show using Lego!

(829) Del Boy's favourite song is Old Shep. Old Shep is a song composed by Red Foley, with lyrics by Willis Arthur, published in 1935. Elvis famously covered this song.

(830) John Sullivan created the part of Boycie specially for John Challis because he had loved John's guest performance in his previous sitcom Citizen Smith.

(831) Christmas Crackers was the first Christmas special and the first episode to be over 30 minutes. It did poorly in the ratings though with 7.5 million viewers - a sharp contrast to the huge figures that later Christmas specials would get.

(832) Roger Lloyd-Pack was the father of the actress Emily Lloyd. Emily was a big star in her youth.

(833) John Challis and David Jason had worked together before Fools and Horses because John was in an episode of Open All Hours.

(834) Years after Fools and Horses ended, both David Jason and John Challis commented that they were somewhat dismayed by the lack of new sitcoms that can be watched by the whole family. Comedies like Peep Show, The Inbetweeners, The Office and Phoenix Nights are all great shows but they are not really something you would want to watch with your parents or children.

(835) David Jason also had a lot of success with ITV during the Fools and Horses era. The Darling Buds of May was a huge hit and David showed what a terrific straight actor he was too in A Touch of Frost. David's deal with ITV was described as a 'golden handcuffs' deal in the early 1990s. He was the biggest star in television.

(836) The writers of Father Ted said that Trigger was a big influence on the character of Father Dougal.

(837) The episode title A Slow Bus to Chingford is derived from the Frank Loesser song (I'd Like to Get You on a) Slow Boat to China.

(838) After the sad death of Roger Lloyd-Pack, David Jason said - "He was a very quiet, kind and unassuming actor who was a pleasure to work with. Although he played the simple soul of Trigger in Only Fools And Horses, he was a very intelligent man and a very fine actor capable of many roles. I shall remember him with fondness and for all the good times we had together."

(839) Del Boy likes leather jackets and polo neck tops.

(840) The character Boycie was based on a second-hand car dealer that John Sullivan used to know.

(841) You could probably describe Del Boy as a workaholic. He is always chasing the next deal.

(842) You can see the influence of Fools and Horses in later sitcoms. Take something like The Office for example. It borrowed the Fools and Horses format of ending with specials and even injected some drama near the end.

(843) A key to the success of Only Fools and Horses is that it appealed to people of all ages.

(844) The nightmare that Rodney has of a future where Damien has taken over the world takes place in 2026!

(845) The replica bar from the Trotter flat sold for £3,800 at a 2021 auction.

(846) Boycie was the name of a man who ran a pub that John Sullivan's dad used to drink in. That name obviously stuck with John Sullivan.

(847) The Jolly Boy's Outing is still the highest rated British sitcom special on IMDB.

(848) Cash and Curry is the first episode where Del calls Rodney a plonker.

(849) Sue Holderness said that members of the public she spoke to often presumed she was married to John Challis real life!

(850) When it comes to business and money you'd say that Arthur Daley is more successful than Del Boy. Arthur has a chic flat and also a warehouse for his goods. He owns properties, drives a Jag, and even seems to own shops from time to time in Minder. You get the impression that Arthur probably has a lot of money stashed away from the taxman.

(851) A rehearsal script for the Jolly Boy's Outing episode sold for £10,099 on eBay. The script originally belonged to make-up designer Dorka Nieradzik - who was the aunt of the seller on eBay.

(852) Del Boy is fond of gold chains.

(853) One of reasons why the BBC had more success than ITV with sitcoms back in the Fools and Horses era is that the BBC had more flexibility when it came to repeats than ITV. If the BBC had a sitcom that hadn't quite taken off they could build up its following by repeating it - sometimes more than once.

(854) David Jason said he wasn't a fan of location shooting in the early days of Fools and Horses because the trailer for the actors was a bit grotty.

(855) A pop up bar which recreated The Nag's Head was opened in 2021 in London. Gwyneth Strong was there for the opening. In addition to beer and Del Boy style cocktails, the bar sold 1980s style bar snacks like cheeselets.

(856) David Jason said the famous scene where Del falls through the bar was done in one take.

(857) The scene where Del falls through the bar had to be nailed in as few a takes as possible because otherwise it would lose surprise for the studio audience and get a smaller laugh and also lose some spontaneity.

(858) David Jason made Del Boy falling through the bar even funnier by the way he doesn't bend or move as he falls. This is a lot harder to do than it looks.

(859) David Bowie is mentioned in the Only Fools and Horses closing theme song.

(860) Despite their similarities, you'd say that Del Boy is much nicer than Arthur Daley. Del Boy is not perfect but he

does have a big heart and a moral compass. Arthur Daley on the other hand can be very selfish and uncaring.

(861) A 'Only Fools and Horses Dining Experience', which toured Britain and featured actors playing characters from the show, was subject to legal action from the estate of John Sullivan for breach of copyright. Deputy High Court Judge John Kimbell QC held that Del Boy is a separate copyright work from the scripts in which he features. This was the first time that the Courts in Britain have recognised that a fictional character can be an independent copyright work

(862) Five of the Only Fools and Horses Christmas specials got viewing audiences of over 20 million. These are incredible figures which would be all but impossible today.

(863) Damien Hodge, who played the adult Damien in a nightmare Rodney has, was married to Tessa Peake-Jones at the time.

(864) If John Sullivan hadn't passed away in 2011 it seems likely that there might have been another Fools and Horses special but it was certainly unthinkable to do one without him.

(865) A young David Thewlis played one of the band members in It's Only Rock and Rock.

(866) David Jason said that him and John Sullivan once turned down an approach from a film company who wanted to do an Only Fools and Horses movie for the big screen. David said the main reason they turned it down was that the company didn't have much money and wanted to do the film on the cheap.

(867) John Sullivan said that Del Boy was a composite of the fast-talking characters he often met working in the car trade in the 1970s.

(868) Buster Merryfield could play the piano a little bit in real life so that was him playing when Uncle Albert tinkles the ivories in the show. The other characters in the show are not the biggest fans of Albert's piano playing skills!

(869) A poll by the website MoneySavingExpert.com saw the public vote for Blackadder and Only Fools And Horses as the two shows they would most like to see come back.

(870) It was actually the boxer Ricky Hatton who purchased one of the Reliant Regal vans from the show for £44,000. Ricky said that in the end he just put the van on display in his garden because it had become too dangerous to drive.

(871) David Jason said that for most of the run of Only Fools and Horses the cast didn't get paid an awful lot.

(872) Nicholas Lyndhurst said he put off accepting the part of Freddie in Rock & Chips because he tends to find that most prequels and spin-offs don't work. He accepted the part though when he read the script.

(873) A UK Gold poll in 2013 voted Heroes and Villains the best episode of Only Fools and Horses.

(874) Del's catchphrase "This time next year, we'll be millionaires!" is first heard in the episode Go West Young Man.

(875) David Jason said that when he was knighted by the

Queen at Buckingham Palace, the late monarch seemed unfamiliar with Only Fools and Horses and genuinely seemed to have no idea who he was!

(876) When he was auditioning for the part of Del Boy, David Jason was asked to do a scene with Nicholas Lyndhurst and Lennard Pearce to see if he had any chemistry with them.

(877) In a 2022 interview for the Radio Times, David Jason said he still misses Only Fools and Horses and playing Del Boy.

(878) Del Boy's favourite cocktail, the Piña Colada, can now be purchased in a can!

(879) Famous people from Peckham include the former footballer Rio Ferdinand and the Star Wars actor John Boyega.

(880) The DVD and later VHS releases of the early episodes of Fools and Horses took out Ronnie Hazlehurst's original theme and replaced it with the familiar John Sullivan replacement.

(881) In 2019, a flat cap worn by Del Boy in the show sold for £3,000 at an auction.

(882) David Jason said that when he, Nicholas Lyndhurst, and Buster merryfield did their skit at the Royal Variety show they all learned one another's lines by heart so that if any of them forget a line the others could prompt them. Thankfully, they didn't have to do this.

(883) In 2019, 31 year-old Daniel Paine from Essex sat

through 50 hours of pain and spent £3,000 to get tattoos of characters from Only Fools and Horses.

(884) Only Fools and Horses superfan Steve Holloway was given an Only Fools and Horses themed funeral by his friends and family in Essex when he sadly passed away in 2022. A Reliant Regal was used as the hearse!

(885) The DJ Mike Read made a guest appearance in It's Only Rock and Roll. That was actually a real recording of Top of the Pops used for A Bunch Wallies television appearance.

(886) The Beckham in Peckham Sports Relief special was dedicated to the memory of Roger Lloyd-Pack.

(887) Daniel Peacock plays 'Mental Mickey' in the episode It's Only Rock and Roll. Daniel had to largely improvise his performance because he was cast at the last minute and didn't have much time to prepare.

(888) Nicholas Lyndhurst said he agreed to play Freddie in Rock & Chips because the character was nothing like Rodney. He said it was fun to play a suave villain.

(889) Rodney is clearly more intelligent than Del Boy and would beat him in an IQ test but Rodney plainly lacks Del Boy's confidence and street smarts.

(890) The website Entertainment Focus ranked Only Fools and Horses as the best British sitcom of the 1980s. They wrote - 'The original run started in 1981, though Only Fools and Horses became a firm favourite with television viewers and a staple of the schedules, especially at Christmastime. It was one of those rare series that had something for

everyone, which is why it occupies the number one spot. Often, whole families would sit down to watch the same show together, and colleagues would discuss the funniest moments with one another at work the following day. Few shows have ever enjoyed such wide appeal. The part of Del Boy cemented the already hugely popular David Jason's status as a national treasure and icon, and he had in Nicholas Lyndhurst (who also starred in The Two of Us – the worst sitcom of the 1980s) the perfect sparring partner.

John Sullivan's depiction of Peckham and working class South East London life is neither too sentimental nor sanitised, but judges it perfectly so that the characters are entirely believable and loveable. Amongst the wider ensemble cast there's plenty of room for broader comic stereotypes, such as the dozy Trigger (Roger Lloyd-Pack) and the sleazy Boycie (John Challis). Always good-hearted, and rarely anything other than hilariously funny, Only Fools and Horses was a phenomenally successful show, and its characters entered the public psyche. "Rodney, you plonker," (and its many derivations) is a catchphrase that will raise a smile for many years to come.'

(891) Despite writing the most famous show in the country, John Sullivan could walk the streets unrecognised and never courted fame or attention.

(892) John Challis said that the new Fools and Horses script John Sullivan was working on when he died revolved around Del Boy celebrating his 65th birthday and everyone gathering at The Nag's Head for Del's retirement bash.

(893) The death of Grandad in the show is generally held up as the moment that Fools and Horses became a comedy drama rather than a conventional sitcom. There is some

terrific 'straight' acting by David Jason and Nicholas Lyndhurst in the Grandad funeral episode.

(894) In 2017, a 'finance expert' said that the Trotter's three bedroom Peckham flat would be worth about £850,000 in today's London property market!

(896) Del Boy falling through the bar was something that David Jason enjoyed performing because he had done this sort of stunt in comic stage shows in the past.

(897) It was reported in 2017 that Fools and Horses is one of the most watched shows on Netflix UK at Christmas.

(898) David Beckham said he was very nervous having to act with David Jason and Nicholas Lyndhurst in the Beckham in Peckham special for Sports Relief. David said he lay awake all night reading the script before they filmed it.

(899) The Jaguar E-Type Series III that Del and Rodney borrow from Boycie in the show sold for £115,000 at an auction in 2016.

(900) There was an attempt at an American remake of Only Fools and Horses. A pilot called King of Van Nuys was written by Scrubs writers Steven Cragg and Brian Bradley in 2012. John Leguizamo was Del with the Rodney character named Donnie and played by Dustin Ybarra. Grandad was played by Christopher Lloyd. This pilot did not result in a series - which is no surprise as it was awful and bore scant resemblance to Fools and Horses. Grandad, for reasons best known to the writers, is a former stuntman in the pilot and Trigger feels more like a character from Breaking Bad than the Trigger we know and love. While the basic concept of Fools and Horses - two working-class

brothers trying to make money - is universal, any English language remake by another country is unavoidably going to lose some of the essence of the show by the mere fact of being transplanted to a different culture. The foreign language remakes work much better than the American one.

(901) The King of Van Nuys pilot was directed by Ted Wass. Wass played Inspector Closeau's nephew in the 1983 film Curse of the Pink Panther. There's some arcane trivia that will never be of any use to you!

(902) When he heard about a proposed American remake of Fools and Horses, David Jason said he was doubtful that Fools and Horses could be transplanted 'across the pond' and still work. Well, he was certainly right about that!

(903) Lennard Pearce appeared on the stage with Laurence Olivier and Anthony Hopkins.

(904) Del Boy's attire in series six is inspired by Michael Douglas in the film Wall Street. Wall Street is a 1987 film by Oliver Stone in which Douglas plays Gordon Gekko - a wealthy, ruthless and heartless corporate raider and financial hotshot. Gordon wore pinstripe shirts and braces. Del Boy doesn't seem to realise that Gordon Gekko is a villain!

(905) John Sullivan had amazing success in the 1980s because he also wrote the classic romantic sitcom Just Good Friends with Paul Nicholas and Jan Francis. John also wrote Dear John - which is not as famous as it should be. Dear John was a short lived sitcom starring Ralph Bates as a man who joins a singles support group after his wife left him. John Sullivan was also involved in the (fairly successful)

American remake of Dear John.

(906) Just Good Friends, which began in 1985, was - unlike Fools and Horses - an instant hit with an audience of eleven million watching the first episodes.

(907) The sitcoms that John Sullivan made in his pomp were beautifully cast - not just Fools and Horses but Just Good Friends and Dear John. Paul Nicholas and Jan Francis have believable comic and romantic chemistry in Just Good Friends and it was a stroke of genius to cast Ralph Bates, best known for sinister horror roles, as the lead in Dear John.

(908) Gwyneth Strong had a reunion with David Jason over on ITV when she played his boss in A Touch of Frost.

(909) Rodney and Cassandra met because they were both on a computer course.

(910) The Robin Flies at Dawn was a five minute 1990 Fools and Horses short film/message that David Jason, Nicholas Lyndhurst, and Buster Merryfield (in character as Del, Rodney, and Albert) made for British troops serving in the 1990–91 Gulf War. This film can be found online - though finding a version with audible sound is another matter.

(911) The Robin Flies at Dawn was shot at an RAF base in High Wycombe. The cast and crew did the short film for free.

(912) Uncle Albert's famous catchphrase is "During the war..." At this point he is usually told to shut up!

(913) The Jolly Boys Outing episode ends with the Chas & Dave song Margate rather than the Fools and Horses theme.

(914) We Buy Any Home calculated that in today's property market you'd have to be considerably richer than Del Boy (before he became a millionaire and was a humble market trader and wheeler-dealer) to be able to afford to rent or buy a flat in Peckham.

(915) The inflatable sex doll episode of Fools and Horses was called Danger: UXB. Danger: UXB was the name of a late 1970s TV show about a bomb disposal team in London during the war.

(916) In the late 1960s, David Jason was in a children's comedy sketch show called Do Not Adjust Your Set. Also in the show were (the then unknown) Eric Idle, Terry Jones and Michael Palin. Because of this, David has said he is still a bit miffed and annoyed that they didn't ask him to be in Monty Python!

(917) David Jason was up for the part of Frank Spencer in Some Mothers Do 'Ave 'Em but was rejected because the BBC didn't think he had 'star quality'. It was obviously Michael Crawford who played this part in the end.

(918) When Rodney is doing his computer class (where he meets Cassandra) the computers used seem to be Amstrad CPC 6128.

(919) David Jason said he took home a lot of Del Boy's clothes from Fools and Horses and still has most of them.

(920) The BBC released an Only Fools & Horses CD ROM in 2000 which had clips from the show plus games and

quizzes.

(921) A YouGov poll found that 93% of the British public have heard of Only Fools and Horses.

(922) In the YouGov poll, 77% of people said they liked Only Fools and Horses and only 6% said they disliked the show. The rest of the people polled were neutral.

(923) The Batman and Robin scene from Fools and Horses was recreated by actors for the opening ceremony of the London Olympics. They jumped out of a yellow Reliant van. I suspect some of the international audience not familiar with the show were rather perplexed by all of this!

(924) The Batman and Robin scene from Fools and Horses was voted the top Christmas television comedy scene in a 2001 poll.

(925) In the episode If They Could See Us Now, Del appears on a quiz show called Goldrush. Del was supposed to appear on the real life ITV show Who Wants to Be a Millionaire? but negotiations between the BBC and ITV collapsed so the fictional show Goldrush was used. A slightly ironic piece of trivia is that Who Wants to Be a Millionaire? was the title of a 1986 Fools and Horses episode.

(926) Another ironic thing is that one of the last Fools and Horses Christmas specials went up against Who Wants to Be a Millionaire? - which was on ITV that night.

(927) Licensed to Drill was a special educational episode of Fools and Horses made in 1984 to show in schools. The story is designed to educate kids about oil and the oil

industry. In the story Del talks about all the uses of oil and then buys an oil rig for £400! This special episode was the last appearance by Lennard Pearce as Grandad.

(928) Appropriately enough, one of the last things Lennard Pearce ever did was make a guest appearance in Minder.

(929) The episode A Royal Flush got preposterously behind schedule due to the cast appearing in the Royal Variety Show and David Jason and Nicholad Lyndhurst falling ill. The episode was still being edited on Christmas morning only hours before it was due to be broadcast!

(930) Although there have been some Fools and Horses 'bloopers' released of the cast flubbing lines, David Jason said they took pride in the fact that there weren't that many outtakes because the actors practiced the material as much as they could before recording to be as prepared as they could. This was obviously important because time is money in the television business.

(931) "This time next year, we'll be millionaires!" was voted as the UK's favorite catchphrase in a 2003 poll conducted by Channel 4.

(932) The laughter from the studio audience during recordings of Fools and Horses was so strong that David Jason often had to pause before his next line.

(933) The BBC very briefly considered casting Wilfrid Brambell as Grandad in Fools and Horses. Brambell was in his early seventies at the time so not actually that old. In the end it was decided that Brambell was too associated with his famous Steptoe character.

(934) Harlech Tower did make a return to the Fools and Horses universe later because it was used in the prequel show Rock & Chips.

(935) David Jason said he thought of Only Fools and Horses as a comedy drama rather than a sitcom.

(936) Another thing that connects Only Fools and Horses and Minder is that the characters in both shows dispense cockney rhyming slang from time to time.

(937) Elizabeth Hurley, who was obviously not famous at the time, auditioned to play Cassandra in Only Fools and Horses. She was rejected because she was deemed too 'glamorous' to be a believable love interest for Rodney. It probably wouldn't be very plausible for Rodney to suddenly turn up with a girlfriend who looked like a Bond girl.

(938) Trigger's real name is Colin Ball.

(939) Only Fools and Horses had a significant impact on British popular culture, with its phrases and characters becoming embedded in everyday conversation.

(940) Some modern retrospectives of Fools and Horses have chided the show for being politically incorrect at times. This is a bit daft and stating the obvious because it is a show which began over forty years ago. Of course it is going to be a bit dated when scrutinised from an ultra PC perspective in 2023. Comedy shows made in 2023 will be dated and perhaps even problematic when viewed in 2063.

(941) John Sullivan's son Jim said the 'PC brigade' will moan about anything these days. Jim thinks that Fools and Horses probably wouldn't get commissioned today.

(942) David Jason said that Jolly Boy's Outing is probably his most cherished Fools and Horses episode - though he finds it hard to pick just one.

(943) Although he is working-class, Del Boy tries to give the impression he is wealthier and more refined than he actually he is. He is also eager to hobnob with the upper classes - which is a comedy trope he shares with characters like Basil Fawlty, Rigsby (from Rising Damp), and Arthur Daley.

(944) It is sometimes said that Buster Merryfield had no acting experience when he joined Only Fools and Horses. This is not strictly true because he had done a lot of amateur stage acting.

(945) Although still very young, Nicholas Lyndhurst was already something of a sitcom veteran when he was cast in Only Fools and Horses. He was in the Porridge spin-off Going Straight and also played Adam (one of the two teenage sons) in the famous Carla Lane sitcom Butterflies.

(946) In the episode The Class Of 62 we learn that Roy Slater is Raquel's estranged husband. As you might imagine, Del is none too pleased about this.

(947) Damien's full name is Damien Derek Trotter.

(948) David Jason and Nicholas Lyndhurst were said to be big pranksters on the Fools and Horses set.

(949) Buster Merryfield sadly died a few years before the last ever specials were made. Uncle Albert's death was written into the specials.

(950) Del Boy has a fear of doctors and dentists and doesn't like visiting them. I think most of us feel the same!

(951) Although there were plenty of working-class sitcoms in the past (Steptoe & Son, On the Buses, Till Death Us Do Part etc), sitcoms were getting quite cosy and middle-class (Yes, Minister, Terry & June, To the Manor Born, The Good Life etc) around the time that Fools and Horses premiered. Only Fools and Horses felt like something different at the time because it was about struggling working-class folk who lived in a Peckham tower block.

(952) The original sheepskin coat worn by Del Boy was purchased on Tottenham Court Road.

(953) The Dutch remake of Only Fools and Horses was called Wat schuift't? ("What's it good for?") The Trotters were called the Aarsmans in the Dutch version.

(954) Grandad did the cooking when he lived with Del and Rodney - despite being a famously bad cook. Uncle Albert also did the cooking when he replaced Grandad in the show.

(955) Roger Lloyd-Pack wasn't supposed to be in Yuppy Love. He had visited the studo that day by chance to inquire when he would next be needed and so - on a whim - was written into the scene where Del Boy falls through the bar. This was a lucky coincidence because Trigger's reaction makes the scene even funnier. Notice how the oblivious Trigger looks slightly startled when Del appears again!

(956) Roger Lloyd-Pack said that The Jolly Boys Outing was his favourite episode.

(957) Though he had worked with Lennard Pearce on the

stage, David Jason hadn't seen him for fifteen years when they were cast in Only Fools and horses.

(958) John Challis said the Batman & Robin scene was his favourite moment in Fools and Horses.

(959) The girl who distracts Councillor Murray before the attempted mugging in Heroes and Villains is played by Sheree Murphy. Sheree Murphy would later become a familiar face on television for her role as Tricia Dingle in Emmerdale.

(960) After the end of Citizen Smith, John Sullivan had an idea for a comedy show set in the world of football. The BBC liked the idea but Bill Cotton, the head of the BBC, decided he didn't want to make it because there was a boxing sitcom called Seconds Out coming out at the time and he didn't want two sporting sitcoms running together. The ironic thing is that Seconds Out starred Robert Lindsay - the star of Citizen Smith. John Sullivan then said his second new sitcom idea was a comedy show about wheeler dealer working class market traders. The BBC liked this idea more and agreed to go ahead. If the BBC had agreed to make the football sitcom then Fools and Horses might never have happened!

(961) The football sitcom that John Sullivan planned was called Over the Moon. It was about a football manager who was past his sell by date and at a struggling club. They actually made a pilot with Brian Wilde (of Porridge and Last of the Summer Wine fame) as the football manager but the BBC decided they didn't want to do this as a series. The pilot for Over the Moon has never been released or leaked - which is a shame as it would be fun to watch it on YouTube.

(962) John Sullivan had written three episodes of Over the Moon when he was told the BBC didn't want to make it. As you might imagine, he was a bit annoyed about this at the time

(963) Joanne Good and Caroline Ellis, who played Nicki & Michelle in Go West Young Man, have both appeared at a Fools and Horses convention.

(964) The Jolly Boys Outing shot a lot of stuff in Margate. They made some use of the famous amusement park Dreamland. Dreamland is close to the train station so hard to miss if you ever visit Margate. Margate is actually becoming quite trendy these days and a bit more bohemian.

(965) The Jolly Boys Outing episode also did some location shooting in Herne Bay. This is another coastal town in Kent.

(966) Like Tessa Peake-Jones, Roger Lloyd-Pack and John Challis were both in Doctor Who. Not at the same time obviously!

(967) Cassandra actress Gwyneth Strong made her film debut as a child actor in the 1973 horror film Nothing but the Night. This film featured a great cast with Peter Cushing, Christopher Lee, and Diana Dors.

(968) Another Kent town used in The Jolly Boys Outing was Broadstairs. They used the old police station there for a scene.

(969) Although the 1997 Fools and Horses Comic Relief sketch was shot after Time On our Hands the Trotters are still at Nelson Mandela House and clearly not millionaires.

(970) Some (though obviously not all) fans consider the last three Christmas specials (If They Could See Us Now, Strangers on the Shore, Sleepless in Peckham) to be a bit unnecessary and annoying because they undo the ending that the characters got in the 1996 Christmas specials.

(971) Uncle Albert doesn't feature in Rock & Chips. John Sullivan said in that timeline Albert was probably away at sea with the Merchant Navy and estranged from his brother (Grandad) anyway. He had planned for Albert to appear in later episodes but John sadly died before this could happen.

(972) John Sullivan said it would have been an interesting challenge finding an actor to play a young Uncle Albert in Rock & Chips!

(973) We never learn what caused Joan Trotter to die at a young age. This would presumably have been revealed in Rock & Chips if John Sullivan hadn't passed away.

(974) David Jason and Nicholas Lyndhurst remained close friends working together on the show. David has said though that he doesn't see as much of Nicholas these days as he would like.

(975) The premise of the Fools and Horses sketch at the Royal Variety show is that Del, Rodney, and Albert are delivering a consignment of hooky booze to a nightclub and stumble into the theatre by mistake.

(976) Del Boy is partial to a Banana Daiquiri. To make this cocktail you mix banana, rum, lime juice, triple sec, and sugar in a blender.

(977) David Jason said that Lennard Pearce lost his temper

one time when he and Nicholas Lyndhurst played a prank on him and had to be calmed down by Ray Butt before he agreed to go back to shooting. David said this was the only time that Lennard got this annoyed over a prank. The prank in question was David and Nicholas nailing Lennard's shoes to the floor in his dressing room so he couldn't pick them up.

(978) Buster Merryfield worked for Natwest Bank for 40 years before becoming a professional actor. He had risen to manager when he retired.

(979) In 1986, John Sullivan had to write new episodes of Fools and Horses, Just Good Friends, and Dear John all at the same time. It was such a challenging task that he often stayed up all night writing to meet his deadlines.

(980) David Jason's portrayal of Del Boy has been praised for its depth and versatility.

(981) Although David Jason said the late Queen Elizabeth II seemed to have no idea who he was when he got a knighthood, other members of the cast said that Buckingham Palace requested advance tapes of Fools and Horses to watch. Maybe it was other members of the royal family who loved the show?

(982) Only Fools and Horses tackles various themes such as family, friendship, ambition, and the dream of a better life.

(983) Only Fools and Horses continues to be celebrated through online fan communities and social media.

(984) David Jason said in one of his memoirs that Open All Hours was exactly like Only Fools and Horses in that it was

largely ignored at first but then became popular through repeats.

(985) Because of his years working in 'civvie street' in a bank, Buster Merryfield once said "I'm in the enviable position of being an actor with a pension."

(986) The Fools and Horses Christmas specials became highly anticipated events for viewers.

(987) Despite their faults, the Trotter brothers are ultimately portrayed as lovable and well-intentioned characters.

(988) The 1997 Only Fools and Horses sketch for Comic Relief has some in-jokes which reference A Touch of Frost and Goodnight, Sweetheart.

(989) Only Fools and Horses was still called 'Readies' on the first scripts that David Jason read. They obviously hadn't come up with the famous title yet - or decided on it at least.

(990) In 2005, in the Queen's New Year Honours, John Sullivan was awarded the OBE for his services to television.

(991) The opening credits to the show were altered three times. The last change was obviously to add Buster Merryfield in place of the late Lennard Pearce.

(992) Elizabeth Hurley was 23 when she auditioned to play Cassandra in Fools and Horses.

(993) David Jason said it was only when he went to a Fools and Horses convention dressed as Del Boy and got mobbed that he truly realised how much the show meant to people.

(994) When the sad news that John Sullivan had died was made public, the BBC's head of comedy said - "No one understood better what makes us laugh and cry than John Sullivan. He was the Dickens of our generation. Simply the best, most natural, most heartfelt comedy writer of our time."

(995) David Jason said that when he first got a script for Fools and Horses, one of the things he was most impressed by was how inventive John Sullivan was in coming up with the sarcastic insults that Del and Rodney exchange in the show!

(996) When it first came out, the Daily Telegraph review of Fools and Horses complained about the "seedy criminality" of the show. Another newspaper review called the people who watched it 'morons' and said the show wouldn't last very long. These critics were made to look rather stupid in the end.

(997) David Jason based Del Boy on a builder he used to work for in the East End of London. The name of the builder was Derek Hockley.

(998) John Sullivan said that the BBC didn't like the first Fools and Horses script but they agreed to make a series because he had a BBC contract to write six episodes of a sitcom - any sitcom. It was either pay him to write Fools and Horses or pay him to do nothing.

(999) David Jason thinks that Only Fools and Horses would be difficult to make to day because television companies want instant ratings rather than shows which take time to grow and build an audience. The world of television is more cut-throat than it was in 1981 because there is so much

content out there fighting for our attention.

(1000) David Jason said that Del Boy is by far his favourite role out of all the characters he has played in his long career.